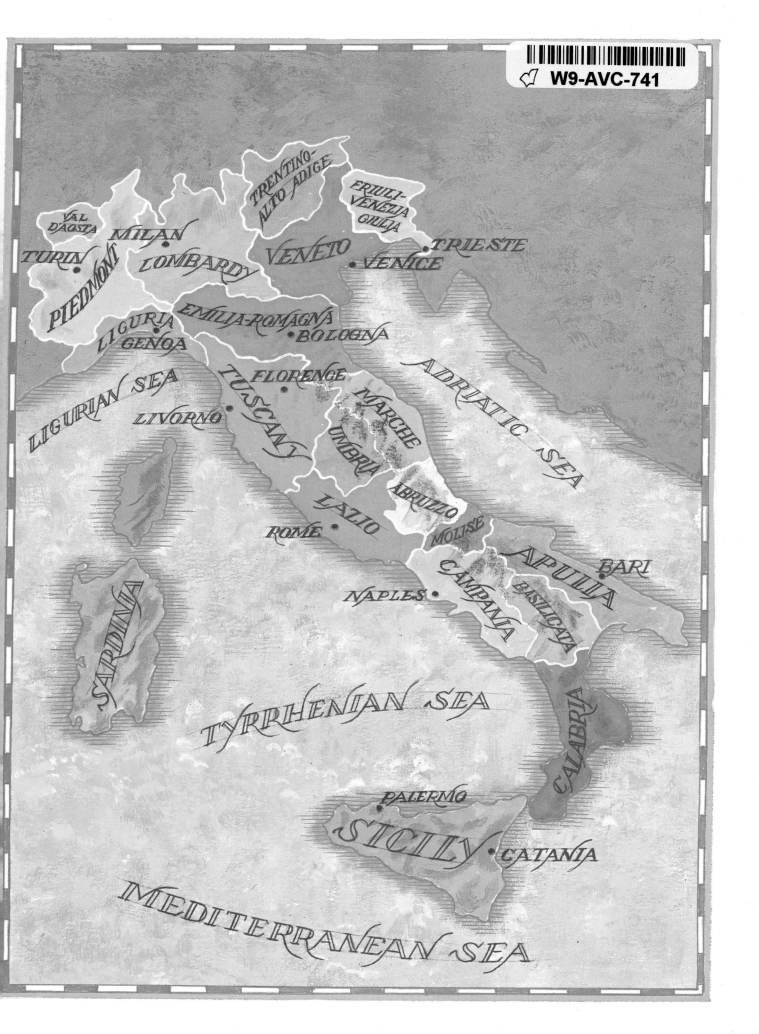

VAL D'AOSTA

TURIN

PIEDMONT

MILAN

LOMBARDY

TRENTINO-ALTO ADIGE

VENETO

FRIULI-VENEZIA GIULIA

TRIESTE

VENICE

LIGURIA

GENOA

EMILIA-ROMAGNA

BOLOGNA

ADRIATIC SEA

LIGURIAN SEA

LIVORNO

TUSCANY

FLORENCE

MARCHE

UMBRIA

ABRUZZO

LAZIO

ROME

MOLISE

CAMPANIA

APULIA

BARI

NAPLES

BASILICATA

SARDINIA

CALABRIA

TYRRHENIAN SEA

PALERMO

SICILY

CATANIA

MEDITERRANEAN SEA

ITALIAN
AMERICANS

ITALIAN AMERICANS:
THE IMMIGRANT EXPERIENCE

Ben Morreale

Robert Carola

METRO BOOKS
NEW YORK

© 2000 Universe Publishing
A Division of Rizzoli International Publications, Inc.
300 Park Avenue South
New York, NY 10010
www.rizzoliusa.com

This 2008 edition published by Metro Books,
by arrangement with Rizzoli International Publications, Inc.

Series Editor: Leslie Conron Carola
Copy Editor: Deborah Teipel Zindell
Design: Ken Scaglia

Metro Books
122 Fifth Avenue
New York, NY 10011

ISBN-13: 978-0-7607-8438-9
ISBN-10: 0-7607-8438-8

Printed and bound in China

3   5   7   9   10   8   6   4   2

A whole nation walked out of the middle ages,
slept on the ocean, and awakened in New York City
in the twentieth century.

Robert Viscusi, *Astoria*

CONTENTS

The gulf of Naples with Vesuvius—once the site of absolute devastation—seen through a soft morning mist.
A great wave of starving emigrants left this land of remarkable contrasts hoping for a better life in America.

INNOBI
LISSIMA
MEDICVM
FAMILIA
MVLTIPRE
CLARIMA
GNIQ3 VI
RIFVERE
INQVIBVS

IOANNES MEDICES·QVI
MAGNO ET·INVICTO Ø
ANIMO VICECOMITIBVS

Sese opponens sæpius patriæ Nostræ
libertatem & communem omnium sa
lutem tutatus est· Verius quoq̃ in
Equestri dignitate· quæ prima apud
florentinos habetur· sine controuersia
princeps· Nostræ quoad uixit Rei ꝑ
extinxit rector et gubernator. Quid Cos
mus Ille Magnus· qui in magnis oli

INTRODUCTION

Italy has been known for being many things—the seat of the Roman Empire, the Mother of the Arts, home to a landscape as interesting and varied as any on earth, centered in the Mediterranean, cradle to some of the most accomplished civilizations in history—but politically, it has been a disaster. Italy is a country without a unifying identity—even today—a country that has had countless foreign rulers in its chaotic history and at least fifty-seven different governments just since the end of World War II. Italy is not only a fragmented country, divided within itself, it is also a country filled with ironies. For example, the great emigrations from Italy to the United States began *after* 1870, when Italy finally became a unified nation. But unification came too late. Italians—especially southern Italians in the *Mezzogiorno* (literally, "mid-day" in Italian, but also used to refer to the south of Italy)—had seen too much misery to ever be optimistic in their own land.

An entire Italian culture left its homeland because it was *morte di fame*—dying of hunger—but even so the people left with mixed feelings. They came to America to become part of the rich weave of life in this faraway land not because they wanted to, but because they *had* to. Unlike their northern Italian neighbors, who emigrated to the United States because they wanted to, bringing with them their education and skills and attracted by the promise of a finer life, the southerners came looking for a place where they could simply survive.

(Previous spread) Piazza S. Francesco Pistoia. Museo Civico, Pistoia, Italy. For Italians, town life has always centered around a central square or piazza. The adaptation of immigrants to their new country was eased by this sense of community.

(Opposite) A page from a Renaissance illuminated manuscript, depicting the life of Lorenzo di Medici, "Lorenzo the Magnificent," incorporates several of the well-loved Italian arts—landscape painting, portraiture, and exquisite calligraphy. The Medici family of bankers ruled Florence, and later Tuscany, almost continuously from 1434 to 1737, and produced three popes: Leo X, Clement VII, and Leo XI.

(Opposite) **A typical street scene at a fountain by the Cappuccini gate in the Sicilian village of Taormina. Women and children at home worked almost as hard as the men in the fields, and found time to gossip, too.**

(Left) **Flower peddlers along a stepped street in Naples, 1902. Emigrants to the United States would encounter even more crowded living conditions as they flooded into urban areas all over the country, forming "Little Italys" wherever they settled.**

These miserable living conditions led to a rebellion in Sicily that lasted from 1892 to 1894. It was called the *Fasci Siciliani,* and was one of the first Socialist movements in Europe. The desperate rebellion was crushed by northern Italian troops, and the young Italians who had spearheaded the uprising decided to emigrate to the United States rather than continue a life that held no promise of a respectable future.

Those early immigrants had no concept of being "Italians." They saw themselves first as Christians, then as people from a particular village or town. A person from Bari was a *Baresi,* from Palermo a *Palermitano,* from Naples a *Napolitano.* It was only in America, thrown in with immigrants from other countries, that the immigrant from Italy found his identity as an Italian. When he stepped onto Castle Garden or Ellis Island the immigration officials there labeled him an Italian, and from then on he was an Italian who happened to be from Naples or Bari. But make no mistake, among themselves, the Italians knew who was from Naples and who was from Sicily, and for a while, Neapolitans tended to marry other Neapolitans and Sicilians married Sicilians.

The real Italian heritage in America began when, once and for all, all Italians were one. Soon enough, second- and third-generation Italians were marrying people from Ireland, Germany, and Poland, even from as far east as Russia. Here is a typical example: Antonio DeGruccio, an immigrant from a farming village outside of Salerno, married Maria Monica Pandaliano in New York City in 1900. Of their eight children, seven (88 percent) married Italians. However, of their eighteen married grandchildren, only four (22 percent) married Italians.

After a two- or three-week-long voyage from Europe, New York City was the main port of entry, and after their official processing at Castle Garden or Ellis Island, most of the Italian immigrants moved into lower Manhattan, which was already crowded with immigrants from Italy and other European countries. From there, some immigrants moved north and east to the relatively wide-open spaces of Harlem, the Bronx, Brooklyn, and Queens, or south across the bay to Staten Island, not yet connected to the mainland of the other boroughs of New York City. Some crossed the Hudson River into New Jersey, where the opportunity to work on a farm gave relief from the hectic life of the cities. Usually, the immigrant went where there was work, most often where friends or relatives had already settled and made some inroads.

When jobs building the railroads in New York State became available, a flock of immigrants moved there. Others headed west, even all the way to the Italian-like farmlands of southern California or the fishing ports of northern California. New Orleans was also a port of entry, and Italians who landed there but did not settle moved onward to Texas and the Mississippi Valley. By 1910, Italians had settled throughout the United States, working in the textile mills of New England; sharecropping in Bryan, Texas; onion farming in Canastota, New York; mining and even organizing labor unions in Colorado; cowpoking in West Texas; lumberjacking in Seattle; and fishing in the rich waters around San Francisco.

The contributions of Italian immigrants and their children and grandchildren have been varied and indelible. There have always been men and

women among Italian immigrants—and their descendants—who set an example. They were often private people who became public heroes, people such as Supreme Court Justice Antonin Scalia, baseball great Joe DiMaggio, Geraldine Ferraro, the first woman to be nominated for the vice-presidency of the United States, and A.P. Giannini, the founder of the Bank of Italy, which became the Bank of America. Heroes continue to be born, and we continue to welcome them.

Immigrants have been coming to the United States since the seventeenth century, but it is only in the last hundred years that so many Italians have left their beloved homeland—over four million alone between 1880 and 1920—to seek the unknown possibilities of a new country that was a wide ocean and a wider culture away. We record their inspiring saga in the pages that follow.

Italian emigrants on their way to a railroad station or seaport usually carried as many of their possessions as they could manage. Undoubtedly, much was left on the dock.

A SHORT HISTORY OF ITALY

The Roman Empire, which began around 450 B.C., was preceded by many non-Italian cultures, including the Greeks. The boot-shaped peninsula that was to become Italy, strategically attractive with its hundreds of miles of coastline jutting out into the Mediterranean, was always in the possession of one or another of these warring foreign powers. Eventually, the Roman Empire grew too unwieldy, having to contend with too many political and military crises, and after almost a thousand years of world dominance, the great Roman Empire collapsed under its own enormous weight in A.D. 476.

(Opposite) **An idealized mosaic with a Byzantine influence, from La Martorana in Palermo, showing Jesus Christ coronating King Ruggero (Roger II).**

ITALY AFTER THE ROMAN EMPIRE

For centuries to come after the fall of the Roman Empire, Italy would once again be ruled by one non-Italian power after another, setting the stage for the eventual emigration of millions of disgruntled Italians in the nineteenth and twentieth centuries. First came the Lombards from central Europe, an invasion and occupation that lasted about two hundred years, and threatened not only the political and economic life of Italy, but also the newly established Catholic Church and its formal leader, the Pope. In an attempt to save himself and the Church, the Pope asked for help from the Catholic Franks, in what is now France.

The Coronation of Charlemagne by Pope Leo III. Miniature from *The History of the Emperors.* Bibliotech de L'Arsenal, Paris. The coronation, with all its pomp and circumstance, on Christmas Day, 800. The Latinized version of Charlemagne's name, Carolus Magnus, means "Charles the Great." His reign as emperor lasted until 814, and melded Christian Rome with the Imperial Rome of Caesar to create the Holy Roman Empire.

Venice c. 1400, showing Marco Polo leaving the greatest of Italy's Maritime Republics. Venice was crucial in establishing Italy's successful sea trade.

Charlemagne led the Franks against the Lombards, and finally defeated the Lombard Kingdom of Italy in 774, adding northern and central Italy to his own kingdom. The Pope crowned Charlemagne as the first emperor of the new Holy Roman Empire (actually neither holy, Roman, nor an empire) on Christmas Day 800. But Charlemagne's unity of Italy was short-lived, as was he. He died in 814, and during the next three hundred years many leaders attempted to head the already-weakened Holy Roman Empire.

At about this time, the Normans arrived in southern Italy and took control from the Lombards and then the Arabs. The system of feudalism resulted,

with the nobles acting almost as princes under the king, each ruling their peasant laborers with their own military forces. Because feudalism was based on the success of an agricultural society, the development of the cities suffered.

The leaders of the Catholic Church became more powerful than ever under feudalism, enjoying a higher status than the nobles. The Church leaders were outranked only by the king. It was this authority that allowed the Pope to initiate the disastrous Crusades, the so-called holy war against the non-Christian "infidels." Christians "took the cross" from Europe throughout the Mediterranean, a campaign that lasted close to two hundred years and cost countless lives. In the end, the Holy Land remained Muslim, and Europeans began to turn their attention westward.

THE SHORT-LIVED REVITALIZATION OF THE CITIES

International sea trade increased toward the end of the Crusades, and the cities began to thrive again. Four of the great Maritime Republics that grew as a result were Amalfi, Pisa, Genoa, and particularly Venice. By the fourteenth century many of the largest European cities were in Italy,

Ippolito Caffi. *Genoa in* 1850. Galeria d'Arte Moderna di Nervi, Genoa, Italy. Genoa was one of the powerful maritime centers of Italy, and the port from which most northern Italians emigrated.

including Venice, Milan, Florence, Naples, Palermo, Bologna, and Rome; each one larger than London.

Italy's sea trade continued to flourish, partly because of its central location in the Mediterranean, but also because it was producing high-quality goods—wool in Milan, cotton in Lombardy, textiles and leather goods in Florence, and silk in the Tuscan city of Lucca. To add to the prosperity, Italian cities began to set the standard in banking, and business in general. The Medici family was the leading banker of Florence, and became a prominent patron of the arts during the Renaissance period from 1400 to 1550, when art and philosophy were almost as important as finance. Today almost three-quarters of European art is in Italy, and almost twenty-five million tourists visit each year, many just to see the original works of Renaissance masters such as Michelangelo, Leonardo da Vinci, and Botticelli.

Foreign rulers continued their domination of Italy in the mid-1500s. Both France and Spain were powerful countries that waged almost ceaseless war for the control of Italy. In 1559 Spain was finally victorious, making Italy a Spanish colony until 1706, with the Catholic Church regaining the power it lost during the Renaissance. As usual, the victors were not interested in the welfare of the Italian peasants, and appropriated as much of Italy's wealth as they could manage. Under Spanish rule Italy's economic position deteriorated badly, with laws and taxes favoring the northern elite, and abusive policies oppressing the masses. The lucrative Italian silk industry was obliterated by heavy export taxes, and a new law allowed taxation by three different parties: the foreign ruler, the landowner, and the overseer. Also, the Spanish managed to keep the nobles and peasants at odds, so that they would not unite against the foreign rulers. Italian initiative was crushed.

In 1706 England, Austria-Hungary, Holland, and Savoy invaded Italy, taking control in 1714. For the next hundred years the greatest influence on Italy came from Austria-Hungary. Italy at that time was actually made up of twelve different countries, each with its own leader, government, laws, language, currency, taxes, and customs. This fragmented political pattern was obviously not uncommon in Italy, and its continuation would have lasting effects on the people in this already beleaguered country. With the end of the eighteenth century came the wave of nationalism that had driven the French Revolution, and this confusing amalgam of "countries" within a country began to shift.

ENTER AND EXIT NAPOLEON

The premise of nationalism was that the people had the right to rule themselves by choosing their own form of government, a concept that had resulted in self-rule for France and the country across the Atlantic to

Lorenzo de Medici (1449–1492) was the most illustrious member of the powerful Medici family, contributing more than any other patron of the arts to the flourishing Florentine Renaissance of the second half of the fifteenth century. His son Giovanni became Pope Leo X.

which Italian immigrants would one day flock. But the Italian people had no leader strong enough to follow the French or American examples, until Napoleon invaded northern Italy in 1796 to fight the forces of Austria-Hungary, France's most formidable foe. Once again, Italy's fate lay in the hands of a foreigner.

Napoleon crossed the Alps during a snowy winter and took less than a year to win the war. He chose Milan as the capital of Italy, now a new country he called the Cisalpine Republic. Napoleon eventually renamed it the Italian Republic, with himself as king. A few years later, Napoleon conquered Rome, took control of the Papal States and ended the Pope's rule, and installed his own brother as the new king. Only Sardinia and Sicily, both islands off the mainland, were not under French rule.

The era of the twelve countries was over, as Napoleon brought the first stages of national unity to Italy. But yet another war and another political upheaval confronted Italy in 1814 as Austria-Hungary, England, Prussia, and Russia combined forces to oust the French from Italy. After

Napoleon's defeat in 1815, the Congress of Vienna restored most of Italy's old boundaries and rulers, Sardinia and the Piedmont region in the northwest the only areas allowed to exist independent of foreign rule. Once again Italy was divided up, this time into eight countries; a change called the Restoration. About 2 percent of the population were able to vote, and they lived in northern Italy. The southern peasants were powerless, and frustrated and despised by their northern neighbors.

Giuseppe Mazzini (1805–1872) argued for the independence and unification of Italy, based on common religion, language, politics, and customs. He believed that the people themselves must create their national unity and that equality of classes was to be achieved through solidified insurrections.

THE RISORGIMENTO: ITALY "AWAKENS"

The next forty-six years were turbulent ones, as Italians in one city after another began to revolt in favor of self-rule. That period, from 1815 to 1861, is known as the Risorgimento, the "awakening," when the idea of Italian unity became a cause that attracted thousands of followers. Italy had always seemed like a country without its own identity, but finally with the Risorgimento, the vision of a new, modern, unified "Italy" seemed possible.

In 1849 Victor Emmanuel II was installed as the king of a new constitutional monarchy, and in 1859 the unification of Italy began. An Italian nation came into existence in 1861, but unification was not complete until 1870. Four men, all from the north, were the main forces behind Italy's unification: Giuseppe Mazzini, King Victor Emmanuel II, Count Camillo Benso di Cavour, and Giuseppe Garibaldi.

Giuseppe Mazzini's main contribution to unification was a philosophical one, early on connecting political change to the idea of unity, and exerting

influence on the dynamic leaders that were to come. His life ended in disappointment when the new Kingdom of Italy turned out to be a monarchy instead of the republic he had envisioned. But Mazzini is now considered to have been one of the true founders of modern Italy. Among those leaders that took up the cause was Count Cavour, who is known as the architect of Italian unification. Cavour, a Piedmontese diplomat, was also the prime minister of Sardinia. He solved the problem of Italian unification by joining forces with France and its new leader, Louis Napoleon, who wanted to lessen the power of Austria-Hungary in northern Italy. The Piedmontese and the French declared war on Austria-Hungary in 1859, and a series of victories led to a full-scale revolution. With the annexation of Parma, Modena, and Bologna, the unification had finally begun.

It was at this point in 1859 that the Piedmontese general Giuseppe Garibaldi (one of Mazzini's early followers) was chosen by Victor Emmanuel to investigate the possibility of adding Sicily to the expanding Kingdom of Sardinia, which included Piedmont. Garibaldi organized a red-shirted volunteer force of a thousand men (the *Mille*) and sailed for Sicily in May 1860. By August his troops, aided by Sicilian peasants, had taken over all of Sicily, and Garibaldi declared himself "Dictator of Sicily." Garibaldi's forces, now enlarged to about twenty thousand, continued their drive northward along the peninsula. But Cavour stepped in again in an effort to defuse Garibaldi's extraordinary popularity, and the king's army was dispatched to Italy to prevent Garibaldi from conquering Rome. The two armies met in October, but conflict was avoided when Garibaldi relinquished his acquired possessions to Victor Emmanuel.

Francesco Hayez. *Cavour.* Brera, Milan. Count Camillo Benso di Cavour (1810–1861) was the first prime minister of Italy, and was influential in uniting Italy under the House of Savoy. A stalemate between the politically controversial Cavour and Victor Emmanuel was broken by Garibaldi's invasion of Sicily in 1860.

In March 1861, Victor Emmanuel declared that all the lands annexed in 1859 and 1860 were to be part of the newly formed Kingdom of Italy. The land belonging to the Catholic Church was seized, but instead of making it available for sale to the peasants it was sold to the already rich landowners. These landowners then proceeded to tear down forests in the *Mezzogiorno* for farming. Instead of creating farmland, the deforestation caused erosion, which created marshy swamps perfect for the breeding of malaria-carrying mosquitoes, which infected about two million southern Italians each succeeding year. Much of the deforested land was still suitable for farming, but because of the threat of malaria the peasants had to live away in the hills, walking several miles to and from the fields every morning and night, which added nonproductive, tiring hours to their already long workdays.

"UNIFICATION"

By 1866 only Rome was an independent state, but it fell to Victor Emmanuel in 1871, and became the capital of the kingdom. In 1859 Victor Emmanuel had ruled less than five million subjects; now he was king to twenty-one million.

Unification was a political reality, but the Italian peninsula had not quite become "Italy." One politician noted at the time, "We have created Italy. Now we have to create Italians." The Catholic Church did not recognize the new nation of Italy, peasants scattered all over the peninsula spoke different dialects and had different customs, and the north remained separate from the south.

When unification finally came it actually made conditions worse for the southern peasants, since the new government was even more efficiently ruthless than the previous one. Farming improvements that had begun to affect the *Mezzogiorno* in a positive way were stopped in favor of promoting industry in the north. Also, protective tariffs benefited the north, while the needs of the south were largely ignored. The typical attitude of northern politicians could be summed up by Cavour's intention to keep the north and south separate in a "unified" Italy. Overtaxation and exorbitant

interest rates became unbearable, and the south was contributing proportionately more revenue to the government than the north.

Caught up in the euphoria of unification, ineffectual politicians spent the country's money trying (unsuccessfully) to establish colonies in Africa instead of focusing on reducing the misery of so many impoverished southern Italians. Whatever form unification was going to take, it was too late to keep the frustrated southerners from leaving home, desperate to find work in other European countries, and soon, across the Atlantic Ocean. Mass emigration was inevitable.

Cesare Maccari. *Meeting at Teano.* Fresco. Palazzo Pubblico, Siena, Italy. In the fall of 1860 Garibaldi met Victor Emmanuel at the bridge in Teano, hailing him as the king of a united Italy after Garibaldi's recent conquest of Naples and Sicily.

Giuseppe Garibaldi (1807–1882) entering Naples in 1860 after conquering Sicily earlier in the year. Garibaldi's continuing conquests eventually resulted in the formation of the Kingdom of Italy in 1861 and the beginning of the reign of King Victor Emmanuel II. His international popularity as a daring leader of his soldiers actually led Abraham Lincoln to offer him a command during the United States Civil War. Garibaldi declined; he wanted supreme command of the Union troops.

Aerial view of the cathedral at Monreale, Sicily. The architecture reflects a distinct Byzantine influence from the early days of non-Italian rule. As usual, the size and location of the cathedral dominates the town, with plains and mountains offering some respite from crowded town life. The Church continued to dominate the lives of Italians—even in the New World—politically as well as spiritually.

BEFORE THE GREAT MIGRATION

I t is ironic that tourists visit Italy in huge numbers, contributing significantly to the Italian economy, while not so long ago Italians left their beloved homeland, in one of the largest migrations in human history, because they could not earn a decent living. Almost thirty million Italians left Italy after the Kingdom of Italy was formed in 1871.

But that is only one of the many ironies that fill Italian history. It was the success of Italian explorers, navigators, mapmakers, and missionaries that ultimately opened the door to immigration and led millions of Italians away from the country they loved first of all. Another irony is that all of these pioneers were sponsored by European nations other than Italy, because "Italy" existed at that time only as a group of independent regions with no central government to support such ventures. As a result, England, France, and Spain gained the early footholds in the New World. What would the United States be like today if many of those early discoveries had been made under the flag of a unified Italy?

THE EXPLORERS

It all started with Cristoforo Colombo (Latinized to Christopher Columbus), the intrepid sailor who made the first Italian–American connection when he left Palos, Spain, on August 3, 1492, and landed at what he thought was

Christopher Columbus
(1451–1506) takes possession
of the New World in the name
of Spain, October 12, 1492,
two months after leaving
Europe. Although Columbus
thought he had reached India
as planned, he actually landed
in the Bahamas.

India, but was actually San Salvador in the Bahamas, on October 12, 1492. (Columbus was born in Genoa about 1451, but not on October 12. When we celebrate Columbus Day it is in remembrance of Columbus's first landing in the New World.)

Columbus believed he could reach India by traveling west directly across the Atlantic Ocean instead of traveling south and then east all the way around the Cape of Good Hope at the southern tip of Africa. Sponsored by King Ferdinand and Queen Isabella of Spain, Columbus made four voyages to the New World, in 1492, 1493, 1498, and 1502, but never actually landed in any part of what is now the United States. The closest he came was Cuba, ninety miles away, and Honduras on the mainland of Central America.

The second of the great Italian explorers was Giovanni Caboto, who Anglicized his name to John Cabot when he moved to England at the end of the fifteenth century. Cabot was also born in Genoa, at about the same time as Columbus, and like Columbus, believed he could reach Asia by sailing west. Anxious to duplicate the successes of Columbus, Cabot began his first voyage in 1496, sailing for King Henry VII in the name of England. The voyage was aborted, but on his second voyage, in 1497, Cabot took possession of Newfoundland for England, and continued his explorations southward. When Cabot returned to England to report his discovery, Henry VII decided to name the newly discovered land New Isle. He changed it to The New Founde Lande (Newfoundland) in 1502.

Although Cabot's northern explorations have been recognized as major contributions, he was never as well known as Columbus, probably because his discovery of Newfoundland did not lead immediately to further British expansion. But it is clear that Cabot's efforts were responsible for the eventual establishment of the British Empire in North America.

Another contemporary of Columbus was the Florentine merchant and navigator Amerigo Vespucci, who actually met Columbus when he was preparing for his third voyage. As chief navigator for the Commercial

(Opposite) **Amerigo Vespucci Mural in the United States Capitol. From 1855 to 1879 Constantino Brumidi (1805–1880) worked as the chief artist for the new U.S. Capitol Building in Washington, painting murals, designing interiors, and sculpting marble statues. He spent almost two years painting the huge mural inside the dome of the Capitol, lying on his back on a scaffold 180 feet above the floor. His signature on the murals reads, "C. Brumidi, Artist, Citizen of the U.S."**

House for the West Indies in Seville, Spain, Vespucci's responsibilities included approving voyages and preparing the maps of any newly discovered lands, as well as the routes to them.

Vespucci himself made two voyages for Spain and Portugal in 1499 and 1501, serving as navigator on the first and then as scientific observer on the second. The first voyage reached the Caribbean, continued to Central America, and sailed past Florida northward along the eastern coast of what is now North America. On the second voyage he explored the north and east coasts of what is now South America, including Brazil and Venezuela, which Vespucci named "little Venice." Vespucci concluded that the lands surveyed on his voyages were not part of Asia, as Columbus had insisted, but were part of a new world instead.

Giovanni Verrazzano (1480–1527) was a Florentine who explored the Atlantic coast of North America.

Vespucci published several popular articles describing his voyages, and a map published by Martin Waldseemuller shortly afterward suggested that the "New World" be named America in honor of Amerigo Vespucci. Although Waldseemuller conceded that Columbus had discovered the Caribbean islands, he thought that Vespucci should be given credit as the discoverer of that southern landmass that Waldseemuller called America, and which is now South America. Later, the northern hemisphere was also called America, hence the names North and South America.

The last of the four great Italian explorers, Giovanni Verrazzano, sailed under the French flag in 1524, and is credited with being the first European to explore the northeast coast of North America all the way up to Maine, sailing into New York harbor

Enrico de Tonti
(1650–1704), pioneering
explorer, is shown in
Texas with a Native
American guide. Tonti
and LaSalle were the
first Europenas (1682)
to explore the Missis-
sippi Valley down to the
Gulf of Mexico.

exactly three months after leaving France. Four centuries later, the new
bridge spanning Brooklyn and Staten Island (areas now heavily populated
by Italian Americans) was named the Verrazzano-Narrows Bridge, now
popularly called the Verrazzano.

Another Italian pioneer in the New World was Enrico de Tonti, a soldier of
fortune, fur trader, and explorer who joined the French military in 1678
for duty in the New World under the French explorer Robert Cavelier de
LaSalle. Tonti and LaSalle explored the Mississippi Valley to the Gulf of
Mexico, with Tonti credited as the founder of Illinois. He also helped open
up the territories that were to become Arkansas, Wisconsin, and Louisiana.
Italian immigrants who settled in Arkansas honored Tonti by naming their
community Tontitown.

During this period of exploration and discovery, only northern Italians
were permitted to travel—the southern Italians were still controlled by the
tyrannical Bourbons—and the northerners made the most of their opportunity. Throughout the countries of Europe the job market was expanding,

Francesco Vigo (1747–1836) arrived in New Orleans in 1774 and soon became a prosperous fur trader who later aided greatly the cause of the American Revolution. A U.S. Postal Service postcard *(above)* honors his contributions.

and the northern Italians carried their considerable skills in the arts to all parts of Europe, helping to build chateaux along the Loire in France, and churches as far away as St. Petersburg, Moscow, and other parts of Russia. Italy had become the "Mother of the Arts."

ITALIANS AND THE AMERICAN REVOLUTION

Many Italians and free-thinkers of other foreign nationalities contributed much to the American Revolution, but none did more than the Italian Americans Francesco Vigo and Filippo Mazzei.

Francesco Vigo was the first Italian to become an American citizen. He was born in Piedmont on December 3, 1747, and as a young man he ran away from home and enlisted in the Spanish army for service in the New World. After being discharged from the army, Vigo accumulated a fortune as a fur trader with the Native Americans, with operations ranging from Detroit to New Orleans and from St. Louis to Pittsburgh and Montreal. His success was furthered by his great linguistic abilities, which enabled him to learn and communicate in several Native American languages. His explorations helped open the Old Northwest for settlement.

When the fighting of the Revolutionary War spread to the Old Northwest, Vigo joined forces with his friend General George Rogers Clark, then commander of the American forces in the West. Later, at age twenty-six, Vigo assumed that command. Besides serving in the army, Vigo contributed funds to buy arms and supplies for the colonists, and he used his friendship with Native American tribes to gain their support for the revolution.

On one of his missions to obtain ammunition and other provisions, Vigo was captured by Native Americans friendly to the English. Because he was technically a Spanish subject, Vigo could not be imprisoned, and he was free to roam around the English fort where he was detained. After Vigo was finally released he quickly reported to General Clark all the information he had gathered while surveying the fort. With this assistance, Clark captured the fort, which was a turning point in the war along the western frontier.

Vigo eventually spent his entire fortune advancing money for arms and supplies, and he died a pauper in 1836. Forty years later the American government awarded his heirs about $50,000 for his aid to the War of Independence as colonel, financier, and intelligence officer.

Filippo Mazzei emigrated to the New World from Florence, eventually becoming a naturalized citizen, an elected official of Virginia, and a fervent supporter of the American Revolution.

The best-known Italian in North America in colonial times was probably Filippo Mazzei, a Tuscan physician who was born in 1730 near Florence. Well educated and acquainted with people in high places, Mazzei eventually settled in London and began importing Italian food, wines, and other products. While in London Mazzei became friendly with Benjamin Franklin, and through him met other prominent Americans including a Virginia statesman named Thomas Adams, who initiated a correspondence between Mazzei and Thomas Jefferson. In 1771 Jefferson, George Washington, and other prominent colonial planters invited Mazzei to come to Virginia to set up an experimental farm. Mazzei sold his London business and traveled back to Tuscany to collect plants and equipment he would need in his experiments in Virginia. He also recruited several peasant farmers to accompany him to Virginia.

41

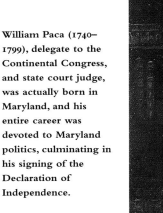

William Paca (1740–1799), delegate to the Continental Congress, and state court judge, was actually born in Maryland, and his entire career was devoted to Maryland politics, culminating in his signing of the Declaration of Independence.

Mazzei and his crew arrived in Virginia in December 1773. On his way to the farm site he stopped at Monticello, and Jefferson suggested he buy a four-hundred-acre estate next to Monticello, and also offered him two thousand acres of Jefferson's own. Mazzei accepted the offer.

The agricultural experiment failed, partly because Mazzei devoted most of his attention to the colonists' growing conflict with England, although he did manage to introduce several Italian vegetables to the colonies. Mazzei became a naturalized citizen of Virginia, and in 1774, he became an elected official there. At Jefferson's suggestion, Mazzei wrote a series of articles supporting a revolution against England, and several ideas and phrases used in those articles influenced Thomas Jefferson and his writing of the Declaration of Independence.

In 1941 President Franklin Roosevelt acknowledged Filippo Mazzei's influence on Jefferson's draft of the Declaration of Independence, and in 1980 the United States Postal Service issued a forty-cent postage stamp commemorating the two-hundred-fiftieth anniversary of Mazzei's birth.

William Paca, the chief justice and governor of Maryland in colonial times, was the only Italian American to sign the Declaration of Independence.

ITALIAN CONTRIBUTION TO ART IN EARLY AMERICA

Constantino Brumidi, the greatest Italian fresco painter to come to the United States, was born in Rome in 1805 and eventually worked in the Vatican for three years before emigrating. Brumidi was a refugee of the revolutionary upheaval in Italy in 1848 and the Restoration of 1849, and emigrated to the United States in 1852, finally settled in Washington D.C., where he worked until his death in 1880.

Brumidi is mentioned in most accounts of the Italian-American contribution to art in America because he painted several large, magnificent frescoes on the ceiling of the rotunda and other parts of the United States Capitol, but many other outstanding Italian-American artists of the early years are usually ignored. These artists include Carlo Bellini, Ferdinando Palmo, Lorenzo Papanti, and especially Giuseppe Ceracchi, the most important Italian sculptor during the colonial period. Ceracchi introduced the portrait bust to America, which was the most important form of sculpture in the early nineteenth century.

Count Luigi Palma di Cesnola. As the American consul in Cyprus, General Cesnola acquired a vast collection of *objets* that he eventually sold to the Metropolitan Museum between 1874 and 1876. In 1879 he was named the first director of the museum.

Thomas Jefferson called Ceracchi "an artist of the first class." Ceracchi was born in Rome in 1751, and before coming to America he worked as a sculptor of prominent citizens in Rome, London, Holland, and Vienna. These statues and busts included likenesses of Sir Joshua Reynolds, Emperor Joseph II, and Pope Pius VI. When Ceracchi visited the United States he completed busts of George Washington, James Madison, Alexander Hamilton, John Paul Jones, and other statesmen.

Count Luigi Palma di Cesnola arrived in New York in 1858 as a professional soldier, but later he would have a tremendous impact on the art world. After his career in the military he was appointed American consul to Cyprus, where he discovered ancient artifacts that he sold to the Metropolitan Museum of Art. As a result of amassing this huge collection di Cesnola was appointed the first director of the museum.

THE MISSIONARIES

What the Italian explorers began, the Italian missionaries continued. Many Catholic missionaries came to America even before the huge wave of Italian immigrants at the end of the nineteenth century. They came, with the blessing of the Church, for two reasons: to bring Christianity to the New World, and to establish colonies for their sponsoring countries. In the process, the early missionaries prepared some of the first maps of the new territories and sent back invaluable information about the New World to Europe.

One of the earliest Italian missionaries was Fra Marcos de Niza, a priest from Savoy in the service of Spain. Fra Marcos came to America about ten years after Verrazzano explored the coast of North America. Fra Marcos explored the territories that would become Arizona and New Mexico, and in 1539 claimed them for Spain.

Another Italian missionary who helped Spain establish possessions in the American southwest was Father Eusebio Francesco Chino, a Jesuit who arrived in Mexico in 1681. A well-known scholar and naturalist, Chino mapped Spain's North American empire from the Colorado River to the

FRAY MARCOS de NIZA F.O.

Fra Marcos de Niza (1495–1558) came to the Americas in 1531, and worked to convert local natives in South America, Central America, and Mexico to Christianity. He erroneously believed he had found the legendary "Seven Golden Cities of Cibola" in present-day New Mexico.

Gulf of Mexico. In the course of mapping the southwest he disproved the prevailing belief that California was an island. Chino's contribution to the economy of the southwest was significant. He established ranchos and mission settlements, helped found the southwest cattle industry, and introduced European livestock, grains, fruit, and vegetables to the region.

Chino died in 1711 at age sixty-seven, having founded at least twenty communities that still survive. In 1965 a statue of Chino was unveiled in Washington, D.C., as a tribute to all the Jesuit missionaries who had the faith and courage to come to a new world.

Father Giovanni Nobili was another Italian Jesuit who arrived in America relatively early. In 1844 he settled in Oregon, and because he was a gifted linguist was able to work with many western and northwestern Native American tribes, each of which spoke a different language. Another Jesuit, Father Joseph Cataldo, came to America in 1860 after being exiled during Garibaldi's occupation of Sicily. He spent sixty-three years among the Native American tribes in Idaho, Washington, Wyoming, and Alaska, learning twenty of the native languages. One of his missions still survives in Cataldo, Idaho, a town named after him.

By 1879 there were 113 Italian missionaries in California. They founded some of the state's first colleges, including Santa Clara and St. Ignatius, and also pioneered the development of California's wine industry.

Only a few Italian immigrants came to America in the seventeenth century. A group of Venetian glassmakers settled in Jamestown, Virginia, in 1622, and by 1632 a small number of Italians had emigrated to Maryland and Georgia. In 1657 the first large group of Italian immigrants came to America, about 150 Italian Protestants seeking religious freedom. The sect, called Waldensians after the founder, a merchant named Peter Waldo, established themselves in the Dutch colony of New Amsterdam. Some Waldensians settled instead on Long Island in an area that became Stony Brook, and a few organized a Dutch-owned farm community in Delaware that was eventually named New Castle. Three centuries later, forty-eight families of Italian Waldensians escaped religious persecution in Italy by founding a community called Valdese in North Carolina, where they eventually established flour, cotton, and hosiery mills.

So, the pattern had been set. Italians were coming to America in search of riches, religious freedom, and adventure. Soon the southern Italians would come by the millions, not just out of a desire for freedom or riches, but in a desperate attempt to survive. They came to America not just for themselves, but for their families, youngsters who had not yet been born. These were the immigrants who would help keep America great.

A day of celebration, complete with American and Italian flags, at St. Joseph's Church in Tontitown, Arkansas, May 18, 1905. Tontitown was the community named in honor of Enrico Tonti, pioneering explorer who opened the Mississippi valley. The Italian ambassador, Baron de Planches (at center with goatee), visits Father Pietro Bandini (seen here to the ambassador's left), founder and priest of Tontitown, and his congregation.

VAL D'AOSTA
TURIN
MILAN
PIEDMONT
LOMBARDY
TRENTINO-ALTO ADIGE
FRIULI-VENEZIA GIULIA
TRIESTE
VENETO
VENICE
EMILIA-ROMAGNA
BOLOGNA
LIGURIA
GENOA
LIGURIAN SEA
FLORENCE
LIVORNO
TUSCANY
MARCHE
UMBRIA
ADRIATIC SEA
ABRUZZO
LAZIO
ROME
MOLISE
APULIA
BARI
CAMPANIA
BASILICATA
NAPLES
SARDINIA
TYRRHENIAN SEA
CALABRIA
PALERMO
SICILY
CATANIA
MEDITERRANEAN SEA

WHY THE IMMIGRANTS CAME

After 1880 about 80 percent of the Italians who came to the United States for a fresh start were from southern Italy. Between 1880 and 1920 the largest percentage of immigrants came from Sicily (29.9 percent), then from the area near Naples (27.4 percent), Abruzzi and Molise (16.2 percent), Calabria (13 percent), Apulia (7.4 percent), and Basilicata (5.8 percent). Why did so many Italians leave the *Mezzogiorno* within such a short time?

(Opposite) A map of Italy, including Sicily and Sardinia, showing the many regions of the "boot." Southern Italy is commonly defined as the area south of Rome. Map by Howard Friedman.

Italy was one of the last nations in Europe to achieve its independence. One foreign army after another had invaded Italy and replaced a sense of pride with a sense of hopelessness, felt most acutely in the poverty-stricken south. An uncaring government (northern Italy was always favored), draft laws that created armies out of young peasant workers who were oppressed by the government they were told to defend, and unfair taxes had all come together to crush the spirit of southern Italians, leaving them only frustration.

At one point in the history of the *Mezzogiorno*, there were twenty-two different land taxes, and by the nineteenth century a landowning elite had provoked the southern peasants, saying, *"Chi ha prato ha tutto"*: Whoever has land has everything. The peasant of the *Mezzogiorno* had nothing but poverty, and it was finally time to do something about it. But few Italians left their homes without regret, reflecting the Italian proverb, *Chi sta bene non si muove*: He who is well off does not move.

The houses most southerners lived in were single-story huts with a loft for sleeping. The ground level was reserved for the animals: a mule, chickens, and for the more fortunate people, a pig. Plumbing did not exist until well into the twentieth century, and farmers dug a hole in the fields for use as a latrine. In some villages an area was set aside as a public toilet. Homes were lighted with kerosene lamps, and most homes had an oven, although the very poor cooked outside on makeshift stone piles. The fuel was straw and twigs gathered in the fall and winter in bundles called *fasci*. Young boys on their way home from their work in the fields usually picked up a bundle of twigs along the way.

A typical single-story house in Sicily, where people and animals might vie for living space. Photo by Diane Hamilton.

A Neapolitan woman in the small kitchen/ sleeping room prepares a family meal on a primitive wood- burning stove. Note the mix-and-match floor tiles, probably garnered one at a time.

Food was simple, if not spartan. There were lentils, split peas, or fava beans, called *macu*, often made into a soup with escarole or wild chicory gathered in the fields. (Many immigrants in the United States continued this prac- tice of picking wild chicory for salads wherever they could find it, usually in empty lots.) On special occasions pasta might be added to dinner. There was usually plenty of fruit, including oranges, plums, apples, lemons, figs, and prickly pears. A family of modest means ate meat twice a year: chicken or a capon for Christmas, and a roasted kid for Easter. It was not surprising that the crowded Italian-American food stores looked like the caves heaped with the treasures of Ali Baba to the disbelieving immigrants.

But for the peasants of the *Mezzogiorno* such gastronomic delights were still far from a reality, and hungry people are not happy people. In 1880, when

A crowded residential section of Naples around the beginning of the twentieth century, where people spent as much time outdoors on their doorsteps as possible. This large-extended-family atmosphere made the future crowded city conditions in America easier to bear.

the flood tide of Italian emigration to the United States began, the average Italian consumed only 28 pounds of meat in a year, while the average United States resident consumed 120 pounds a year. Only Portugal had a lower ratio of meat consumption than Italy. (Many first- and second-generation Italian Americans from the *Mezzogiorno* continued to eat a high-carbohydrate, low-protein diet out of habit, which probably contributed to their generally small stature and that of their immediate descendants.) At the same time, Italy had a *deficit* of 5 million bushels of wheat, while the United States had a *surplus* of 150 million bushels, probably yet another inducement for pasta-loving Italians to emigrate to the United States.

The seeds of rebellion had been sown, but not the seeds of wheat, and it was beans that filled the stomachs of the hungry Italians. (Well into the twentieth century, Italian Americans would still be happy to make a meal of beans, cooked celery, and small pieces of bread in a meatless stew, or to enjoy a continuing favorite, *pasta e fagioli*, pasta and beans.) Farmers in the *Mezzogiorno* grew whatever vegetables they could, not for sale, but for their families. In the 1880s bread riots broke out in many Italian cities and rural areas, including Calabria and Sicily. (As usual, children seemed to find a way to turn lemons into lemonade; Sicilian children, who worked twelve hours a day in a lemon factory for ten cents, used a lemon to play soccer.)

Italy could not have stood further calamity, but it came anyway. Between 1884 and 1887 cholera epidemics killed fifty-five thousand people in Italy, providing yet another reason to leave.

At the same time, the already precarious economy of Italy was shaken by the increased production of citrus fruits in California and Florida, along with improved methods of production, sales, and transportation there. The citrus farmers in Calabria, Basilicata, and Sicily could not compete. To make matters worse—it all begins to sound like a biblical disaster story— natural disasters added to *la miseria*. Earthquakes, landslides, drought, and excessive heat were aggravated by an infestation of plant lice called *phylloxera* that destroyed most of Italy's wine industry, increasing French tariffs on Italian wines and allowing French wines to seize the overseas market. Two of Italy's most profitable export markets, the United States and France, had dried up. Farm laborers left in droves.

Two other crucial factors that contributed to the mass emigration from southern Italy were the climate and terrain. Although we have been conditioned to think of "sunny Italy," the *Mezzogiorno* was far from the perfect place for agriculture. In fact, most of the terrain was mountainous—too high for farming and too low to supply melted snow to irrigate the valleys below. In fact, Italy is the most mountainous of the great European countries. Secondly, most of the rainfall came in the winter, when it mainly caused erosion, not in the spring or summer when the rain was needed to nourish the crops. Also, rainfall in southern Italy was totally unpredictable, ranging from drought to floods. The beloved soil was strangling the peasants who tilled it.

One of the gifts the new regime bestowed on all Italians as a result of unification was the right to travel wherever and whenever they pleased. Yet there was little immediate indication that Italians had any intention of leaving the country in large numbers. In 1870, Ercole Lualdi, a member of the Chamber of Deputies, did, however, warn that Italians were beginning to leave the country in significant numbers. "Do not delude yourselves into thinking that these people are leaving in search of riches," Lualdi told his fellow government officials. "They are leaving in tears, cursing the government and the *signori*." He was right. Only a few years earlier, northern Italy accounted for 85 percent of the annual emigration from Italy. Now the massive emigration from the south had begun. It would bring to America the most downtrodden white people that had ever set foot there.

WHAT IS THE *MEZZOGIORNO*?

A difference between northern and southern Italians, and northern and southern Italy, will probably persist forever. Exactly where does the south— the *Mezzogiorno*—begin?

(Opposite) **One of the many outdoor bread peddlers on the streets of Naples. Bread, not meat, was an everyday staple.**

For residents of Rome, the south begins near Naples. If you live in Florence, the south begins at Rome. Italians in Bologna or Milan see the south as starting in Florence and extending all the way down to the tip of the boot. All versions of the *Mezzogiorno* include Puglia, Calabria, Basilicata, Sicily, and Sardinia.

Objective mapmakers usually depict the northern border of the *Mezzogiorno* as Naples, which includes about 35 percent of Italy's total land area.

At the end of the 1870s an average of almost 118,000 Italians, chiefly farm workers, emigrated to other countries every year. While peasants of the north were able to resettle in northern Italian cities, there was not room enough for the peasants of southern Italy as well. Besides, northerners did

A 1906 Italian poster advertising insurance in case an emigrant died within thirty days of embarkation from port, in this case Naples. Insurance could also be purchased for the reimbursement of the ticket cost if admittance into the United States was denied.

not want southerners coming into their territory. By the end of the nine-teenth century more than 5.3 million Italians had emigrated, nearly half a million more than Italy's population grew during the same period. A year before Garibaldi died in 1882 he lamented, "It is a different Italy than I had dreamed of all my life, not this miserable, poverty-stricken, humiliated Italy we see now, governed by the dregs of the nation." Garibaldi deplored the disaffection of the peasants and attributed it to Italy's failure to produce enough grain to feed its people.

Emigration from Italy was not a new phenomenon, but it was soon to reach new heights, with southern Italians vastly outnumbering those from northern Italy. By 1880, just before the great waves of Italians left their homeland, approximately forty-four thousand Italians already lived in the United States, with over ten thousand of them living in New York City.

From 1800 to the late 1890s most Italians emigrated to South America (especially Argentina and Brazil), Switzerland, Germany, and Austria, the majority of them males from the north of Italy who intended to return to Italy, usually making the Atlantic crossing more than once. Emigration to South America was especially attractive, largely because of the similarities between the two regions—climate and geography were familiar, related languages (Spanish and Portuguese) were spoken, the "Mediterranean" temperament was common to both areas, resulting in less discrimination toward the newcomers, and Catholicism was the dominant religion in both South America and Italy. The Italian immigrants were actually welcomed in South America, and as a result enjoyed quicker upward mobility than in North America.

Around 1850, Argentina and Brazil were attracting Italian wokers. Here the seasons were the opposite of those in Italy. So the Italian farmers could work on their own land until the harvest season was over in October or November, and then work on South American farms for the other six months, returning to Italy in time for spring planting at home.

The men who traveled back and forth from Italy to other countries for seasonal work were called "swallows" or "birds of passage." These diligent workers were resented by Americans, who mistakenly considered their behavior a weakness in Italian character. Some birds of passage might go back and forth as many as four or five times, but eventually most of the southern birds of passage would return to the United States for good, often having earned enough money to bring their families to the promised land with them. Only at the turn of the century did whole families make the one-time trip to the United States together.

The earliest birds of passage, at the beginning of the nineteenth century, had made their way across the Alps from northern and central Italy, doing seasonal work as farmhands, laborers, masons, or stonecutters, and then returning home again. The southern Italians would begin to leave home for seasonal work later in the century. After a while the northern and central birds of passage began to branch out, helping to build railroads in the Balkans, Russia, and North Africa, and working on the construction of the Suez Canal. Little by little, some workers remained where they worked, and Italian settlements began to spring up all over Europe and the Mediterranean basin.

Between 1861 and 1881 about 120,000 Italians emigrated to other countries permanently, but most of these were still northern Italians. About 90 percent of Italians who emigrated to South America were northerners; about 90 percent who emigrated to the United States were southerners. But the status of the two entering groups was completely different. Many northern Italians, artisans and merchants in their homeland, became professionals, and helped to establish Italian colonies, not only in South America, but in the United States, Algeria, Tunisia, and Egypt as well. But the northern Italians' disdain for southern Italians was so intense that the northerners even persuaded the United States government to keep separate statistics for themselves and their poor relatives from the south.

Weaving utilitarian baskets on the wharves in Naples can be a mixed blessing—lonely yet satisfying.

LEAVING THE *MEZZOGIORNO*

The surge of emigration to South America suddenly switched to North America in the 1870s and 1880s when an outbreak of yellow fever in Brazil killed about nine thousand Italian immigrants there. The epidemic caused the Italian government to temporarily halt emigration to Brazil, and at about the same time many Italians decided not to travel to Argentina or Paraguay because of uncertain political and economic conditions there. By the 1890s the United States had also become the favored destination over European cities.

Once again, irony appears in the circumstances surrounding Italian emigration. The mass exodus to the United States actually helped relieve Italy's economic problems by decreasing the Italian population, and Italian immigrants helped the economy further by diligently sending money back to their relatives in Italy. (In 1901, each working Italian immigrant sent home about $250, in addition to gift packages of all kinds. By 1914, Italian immi-

(Right) Long strings of spaghetti hung out to dry on specially built racks are checked by Neapolitan inspectors.

(Opposite) San Gimignano, a medieval town with thirteen towers remaining from its original seventy, photographed on a more recent laundry day. Photo by Erich Lessing.

grants had sent more than $700 million to relatives in Italy. Now the rest of the family could emigrate too.) In addition, Italian Americans helped Italy's sagging export market by buying Italian foods and other products manufactured in Italy.

But there was a negative side to emigration too, especially in the *Mezzogiorno*, as usual. With so many young farmers leaving, Italian farms went unattended, and women and children tried desperately to do the work of the absent males. Also, because most of the early emigrants were healthy males between the ages of fifteen and forty-five, Italy's military forces suffered a serious decline.

The *Mezzogiorno* would lose its most adventurous and courageous residents to the United States, where the Statue of Liberty would be the symbol that welcomed them to a new life—a life that might really bring a chance at happiness. The immigrants wanted at least that.

THE PAINFUL PASSAGE

If the millions of Italians who emigrated to the United States had known how wide the Atlantic was they may never have thought about leaving the land they knew, but these Italians were not just hungry, they were brave. Events they could not control had forced this decision upon them, and had brought them to this strange world of a steamship, for the emigrants couldn't just go from their Italian village to an American city—which would have been enough of a shock—they had to get aboard a ship.

(Opposite) **These non-smiling travelers are aboard ship en route to the United States, "the land of opportunity," after an earthquake in Italy left them homeless.**

TO THE SEA

The first step away from the village was toward a seaport, probably Naples or Genoa. Italians made their way to seaports any way they could. Some walked, some loaded family and baggage into a rented horse-drawn cart, those who were farthest away and could afford it took the train. No matter how they traveled, all these displaced pioneers carried all their possessions with them. (Italians seemed to prefer to take along their bedding and feather mattresses.) Everyone, even the children, carried something. If a mother held a child in each hand she carried a package with her teeth. Of course, these reluctant travelers probably did not have too many possessions to choose from—more difficult was leaving familiar customs behind, and the land that had forsaken them.

Naples was the main Italian port of exit overseas; others were Genoa, Palermo, and Messina. During the peak travel years more than a dozen steamship lines offered a direct passage between Naples and New York City. Not all companies were Italian, and it was a peculiar—but common—sight to see hundreds of Italians walking up the gangplanks onto foreign ships. The foreigners were still making money off the Italian peasants.

The immigrants left with hope and sadness at the same time, trying not to look back. When they reached the Italian seaport they probably saw more people and more bustling activity than they had ever experienced in their home village, a precursor of what was to come in America. Some—maybe most—of these travelers were smelling the ocean for the first time, a smell that evoked both joy and fear.

While the travelers waited for their ship to leave they shared lodgings with dozens of other emigrants if they could afford the few pennies it cost, or else they spent the nights in the streets, careful not to be swindled by ticket sellers and other "concerned" countrymen, who preyed on these naive, disoriented pilgrims. In Naples peddlers sold so-called American clothes, false certificates for smallpox vaccinations, and cures for trachoma, a contagious eye disease that caused the rejection of many immigrants upon their arrival at the processing stations in the United States. Other con men dressed as monks and priests sold pictures of saints that would assure a safe passage. A "porter" took your suitcases and promised to deliver them to your "cabin," and promptly disappeared.

The seaport was not a place where the inexperienced travelers wanted to dawdle, especially since they didn't have any extra money to spend while waiting—sometimes days during the early periods of immigration—for their departure. But by the end of the nineteenth century regular and reliable ship schedules were usually available, and emigrants needed to spend less time waiting in the seaport.

From 1891 on, the shipping companies at the ports of exit were responsible for vaccinating, disinfecting, and examining all passengers before they left port. But few companies performed more than cursory examinations, and as a result many immigrants who could have been detained and possibly cured in their home countries were rejected upon reaching the United States. Strangely enough, Italian shippers were the exception, because of the diligence of Fiorello H. LaGuardia, a future mayor of New York City, who was then a young American consul in Europe. LaGuardia insisted that Italian steamship companies perform their medical duties carefully, thereby avoiding the inevitable disappointment many immigrants felt when they were rejected in America and sent back to Italy.

After World War I several other European countries followed the Italian model, making sure that pre-boarding examinations were thorough, and in 1924 the United States required complete medical examinations before ships left for the United States.

"Addio, Italia!" Emigrants aboard the Italian ship *Duca di Savoia* wave an emotional farewell as they leave Naples for the United States.

CROSSING THE OCEAN

Emigrants crowd onto the deck of the ocean liner *S.S. Patricia* for a group portrait, about 1906. Although transatlantic living conditions were generally poor for third-class passengers, this crowding is exaggerated for the benefit of the photographer.

Finally aboard ship and underway, the next phase of the journey faced the reluctant traveler: the crossing itself. As time went on it took less and less time for a steamship to cross the Atlantic, but it was usually best to expect the trip to take two or three weeks. The crossing required not only a strong spirit, but also a strong stomach.

Most immigrants traveled third-class, or "steerage," so-called because their quarters were below deck next to the steering mechanism and engines.

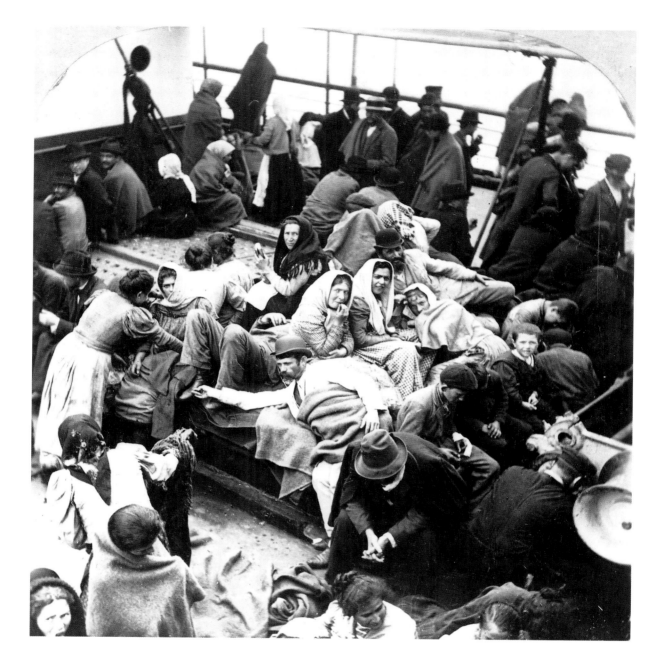

Steerage fare was usually between fifteen and twenty-five dollars. If an immigrant could afford it, it was certainly worth traveling second-class instead of steerage. (Almost no immigrants traveled first-class.) Not only would second-class passengers avoid the crowded, smelly, windowless confines of steerage, they would in addition be admitted into the United States without a rigorous inspection. Occasionally a family would send a sick relative via second-class while they themselves traveled below in steerage to avoid a medical examination of the sick person upon arrival.

Weary shipboard travelers took every opportunity to emerge from their below-deck living quarters in the steerage section to an allocated portion of the open-air upper deck.

The steerage section held between three hundred and six hundred people. It was virtually the same as the baggage compartment: no portholes or other ventilation; low-ceilinged, narrow corridors; crowded spaces for triple-layered bunks with thin, coarse mattresses, if any at all. Men and women were separated, sometimes only barely by a sheet hung over a rope, and the stifling smells of oil lamps and ceaseless engines, later to be accompanied by the unmistakable odors of vomit and urine, not to mention fear, were constant. Food was poorly prepared and infrequently served, consisting mostly of herring, barrels and barrels of herring that cost the shipper almost nothing but could still keep a person reasonably healthy for a couple of weeks. Fresh water was available only on deck, and toilets were inconveniently located. Seasickness was common night and day—some immigrants too sick to eat existed on water alone—and there was crying, crying all the way. Some immigrants were detained at Ellis Island for the eye disease trachoma when they merely had red eyes from their constant crying.

Some people were seasick the entire crossing. The only open deck space available was usually small, and situated in the direct line of soot from the smokestacks. When the steerage passengers were allowed to take turns going on deck to stretch out their cramped limbs, a harsh wind might spoil the moment by blowing a favorite hat overboard. The children were gripped tightly.

For many, the steerage passage across the Atlantic was remembered as a kind of purgatory, viewed as a period of severe punishment imposed on them by Providence for having abandoned their motherland. They prayed that they would reach "*lamerica*" soon, where they could sit in the open air eating a piece of bread, watching their children play.

Then one day the magic words were passed: "*Lamerica! Lamerica! Statua Liberta!*" They had finally arrived, and they all rushed up to the deck, still crowded but not noticing now. All crowded on one side so they could get a good look at *La Statua Liberta* (the Statue of Liberty was erected in New York Harbor in 1886), they watched as the ship glided slowly past the Statue of Liberty and even Ellis Island. Wasn't the ship going to stop? But the

An Italian family arriving in New York harbor in 1905 after a long, difficult journey. The package on the man's shoulder probably contains everything they own. Notice that the children have been dressed in their best clothes to make a good impression on arrival. Photo by Lewis Hine.

(Left) A vision of melancholy—and perhaps a touch of seasickness? This elderly Italian woman can only have mixed feelings as her ship approaches Ellis Island in the early twentieth century.

(Opposite) First- and second-class passengers arriving at Ellis Island in the early 1900s undergo an inspection of their baggage under privileged conditions. Steerage passengers went through a much greater detention period and more rigorous inspection upon arrival.

ship did not stop, continuing through the bay into the Hudson River and northward to a pier on the west side of Manhattan. Resentful steerage passengers could only watch as the first- and second-class passengers were allowed to bypass Ellis Island, disembarking directly from the ship into New York City. The steerage passengers could glimpse New York, and behind them across the Hudson, New Jersey. Teased with only that glimpse, they

W. A. Rogers.

would not be allowed to disembark yet. They had been given a peek at the New World, but now they were pulled back to the reality of the third-class immigrant, and they wondered: Will we ever set foot in *lamerica*?

Writer Mark Helprin, in his novel *Winter's Tale*, describes the ambivalent feelings of poor European immigrants as their ship arrives in New York Harbor:

> The immigrants could almost hear music as the buildings rose up ahead and sparkled. Here was a place that was infinitely variable and rich. Its gates were like the gates of heaven; and if there were some on the other side who said that this was not true, all one had to say was, "After what I have been through, the power of my dreams makes it true. Even if this place is not the great beauty that I think it is, I'll make it so, one way or another." As they moved in the packed line, they looked over the rails and saw people beyond the barriers smiling at them as if to say, "Just wait! You have hard and good times ahead, as I did." The signals were from everywhere and very strong. The world they faced was terrifying and beautiful.

ELLIS ISLAND

When the first- and second-class passengers had finally been unloaded, the ship moved away from the pier and headed back down the river to the deep waters just beyond Ellis Island. From there the immigrants were loaded onto ferries that would carry them to Ellis Island, where their final processing would begin. If dark had fallen in the meantime the immigrants would have to wait until the next day to leave the ship. If the ship arrived on a Saturday it would wait in the harbor until Monday before the passengers were unloaded, or if there were other ships already waiting to unload their steerage passengers, the immigrants might have to wait several days before a ferry was available to take them to Ellis Island. (After 1880 as many as fifteen thousand Italian immigrants reached the United States daily.) Next to being sent home, this unexpected delay must have been the most frustrating experience of all.

(Opposite) **An Italian mother and her three children huddle together on their arrival at Ellis Island in 1905, a particularly busy time for Italian arrivals. Photo by Lewis Hine. Photo © Corbis-Bettmann.**

When their turn finally came, the waiting passengers were ferried to Ellis Island, where they were examined and processed, usually in one day. No matter what part of Italy the immigrants came from they all had something in common when they were finally deposited on Ellis Island: physical and emotional exhaustion. Most of them had managed to survive the worst the ocean could deal them—most adults were, after all, in their physical prime—but now they had to go through yet another ordeal. It was one crisis after another. They didn't know exactly where they were or how long they would be there, they didn't know if any members of the family would be rejected and sent back across that awful ocean (it would not be surprising to believe that *every* immigrant expected to be rejected), they were surrounded by strange people in military-looking uniforms who spoke a strange language, and the average family had less than twenty dollars stashed away in a deep pocket.

One of the most common reasons for rejecting immigrants was the contagious eye disease called trachoma. As a result, every person arriving at Ellis Island was given a thorough, and frightening, eye examination by immigration officials using metal hooks.

They were scared, and they were tired. But they would not allow themselves time to recuperate. They had to be strong to leave their homes, and that strength would have to see them through whatever obstacles lay ahead. They would catch their breath, spend a few hours reuniting with friends and relatives who had come before them, and then they would start looking for work. They could not permit themselves to forget that was the reason they had come.

Once on Ellis Island and inside the main building, uniformed men pinned identifying tags to the immigrants' clothing and the travelers were told to leave their baggage on the main floor (no doubt a moment of intense fear, wondering if they would ever see their treasured possessions again) while they were directed up a flight of stairs holding their identification papers and sporting their large white tags. At the top of the stairs doctors watched the immigrants closely to see if they could detect any obvious physical problems that would automatically reject the person. (After 1911 the medical examination took place on the main floor, and men and women were separated until the examinations were complete, which added to the already high level of anxiety; children were sometimes isolated from their parents,

Immigrant children in the clearly Americanized playground at Ellis Island, 1905. Immigrants were often detained on Ellis Island for several weeks, and officials tried to make the stay as painless as possible, at least for the children.

A CLOSER LOOK:
ELLIS ISLAND

Ellis Island, famous for being the point of entry for immigrants, actually did not open until January 1, 1892; although it was still unfinished, seven hundred immigrants stepped inside that day.

In the 1600s Ellis Island was originally called Kioshk, or Gull Island, by Native Americans. In the early 1700s it was called Gibbet Island, because condemned criminals were hung there from a gibbet, or gallows tree. Later in the 1700s the island was known as Oyster Island because there were so many shellfish in the surrounding waters. The name Ellis Island wasn't used until the early 1780s, when the merchant Samuel Ellis bought the island and gave it his name.

Ellis Island was purchased by New York State in 1808, and it was used as an ammunition dump until January 1, 1892, when it was opened as an immigrant-receiving facility. (Fifteen-year-old Annie Moore from Cork, Ireland, was the first immigrant to be admitted to Ellis Island; the last was a Norwegian merchant seaman in 1954, just before Ellis Island was closed.) Some of the corruption that had supposedly been eradicated at Castle Garden still persisted on Ellis Island, and it soon became evident that some immigration officials there were not treating the immigrants fairly. In 1901 President Theodore Roosevelt fired the commissioner of immigration and other top immigration officials, and ordered sweeping changes that finally gave Ellis Island the decent image it deserved.

In 1897, just five years after Ellis Island opened, a fire broke out and destroyed all the original wooden buildings, but all 140 immigrants on the island, along with immigration employees, escaped unharmed. The rebuilding of a new fireproof facility began within two months, and the new main building—as it looks in its restored version today—was reopened on December 17, 1900.

(While the new Ellis Island facility was being built immigrants were processed once again at the Barge Office at the lower end of Manhattan.) *The New York Times* praised the new building: "One has only to remember the old ramshackle structure to appreciate the magnificent and admirably arranged new quarters. Situated on one of the most prominent locations in the harbor, the new station is an imposing as well as a pleasing addition to the picturesque waterfront on the metropolis."

Additions to the new Ellis Island facility soon became necessary because of the huge influx of immigrants from all over the world—between 1901 and 1910 almost nine million immigrants passed through, over two million from Italy alone—and in 1903 two more landmasses were connected to Ellis Island. (More than twelve million immigrants of all nationalities came through Ellis Island; that number does not include more than four million other travelers who arrived as first- or second-class passengers. All together, more than one hundred million Americans have ancestors who passed through Ellis Island.) The landfill for one of the additions came from the dirt excavated from the new IRT (Interborough Rapid Transit) subway system in New York, which Italian immigrants had helped build. The new building housed mostly hospital facilities.

During the sixty-five years that Ellis Island was in operation, 355 babies were born there as United States citizens, but more than 3,500 immigrants died there, including 1,400 children. It is with good reason that Ellis Island was known as the Island of Hope to some, and as the Island of Tears, or Hell's Island, to others.

Ellis Island was closed in 1954, but in 1992, the one-hundredth anniversary of Ellis Island, the deserted, rundown facility was restored and reopened to the public as a historical museum, where the children and grandchildren of immigrants could see for themselves, and show their children, where it all began.

and screaming babies could be heard throughout Ellis Island, yet another contribution to the immigrants' harrowing experience.)

The medical examiners placed chalk marks on any immigrant who showed some apparent disability that would have to be checked more thoroughly later. If you received a dreaded chalk mark you were detained for a more thorough examination, usually staying at Ellis Island overnight. Passengers who were detained had their first chance to sample American food, an improvement over shipboard fare, and if nothing else it was plentiful; it may even have included the first sandwich the immigrant had ever had.

The medical examinations were usually perfunctory ones, since about five thousand people passed through Ellis Island each day during peak years. (In 1917 the United States tightened its examination procedures, and instead of four thousand or five thousand immigrants being processed in a day, only two thousand or three thousand could be passed through.) Usually only the most obvious ailments were uncovered, and only a very small percentage of immigrants were actually rejected. After that examination came a verbal examination, and the immigrants moved on to the central room called the Great Hall or Registry Room, a large, imposing space two hundred feet long, one hundred feet wide, and fifty-six feet high. To those immigrants who had just spent two or three weeks in claustrophobic steerage quarters, the ceiling must have seemed as high as heaven itself.

The Great Hall was divided into narrow spaces to help create a sense of order. These cubicles held about thirty people at a time, who sat inside the fenced-in cubicle silently waiting to be called, their large identification tags seemingly more important than their faces. Rimming the Great Hall was a balcony, from which hung a huge American flag.

During the verbal examination the immigrants were questioned by a new set of uniformed officials about their job status, amount of money in hand, final destination, waiting relatives, criminal records, and other such matters, and were checked against the ship's manifest, a huge sheet of paper that the interviewer spread out on the table in front of him. It was common at that

(Opposite) **A hopeful Italian family gazes at the Statue of Liberty from their arrival point on Ellis Island. The first sight of the "Lady in the Harbor" usually filled the tired immigrants with a mixture of sadness and elation.**

A mother and child detained and then rejected after their pre-entry examination. All rejections were heart-breaking, especially after the ordeal of leaving Italy and crossing the Atlantic.

point for complicated names to be changed to simpler ones. Few immigrants complained about changes in their names, so anxious were they to pass through Ellis Island without incident. Italian-speaking interpreters helped to ease tension.

Immigrants had to be especially careful when answering questions about their job status. If they said they had a job waiting for them they could be considered *contracted labor*, and sent back to Italy, and if they said they had no job prospects they could be rejected as being potential public burdens. They carefully rehearsed answers such as, "I have good job prospects," or "My cousin will help me find a job."

This now famous space on Ellis Island called the Great Hall or the Registry Room
organized hundreds of immigrants at a time into small groups as they awaited processing.
Note that the American flag, hanging from the balcony, has only forty-six stars.

If the information supplied to the examiner was consistent with the ship's manifest, and no other problems were discovered, the examination was over, and the immigrants were free to go. They had passed through Ellis Island without a hitch, and they stood still for a moment, looked around them in shock, and all asked themselves the same question: *Now* what happens to me?

They would soon find out. They were told to walk down a corridor to a door bearing the simple, yet emotion-filled sign, "Push. To New York." Indeed, they would find that to make it in New York they *would* have to push. For now, they felt a moment of relief as they passed through the door to the cheering reception of waiting friends and relatives, and then there was yet another ferry ride for their long-awaited trip to Manhattan—*lamerica*—or, guided by immigration officials, to a train that would take them to some other destination. Of course, they still could not believe it, but the tears of joy that cascaded down their pale cheeks spoke for them: At last, thank the Madonna, they had made it.

Two young Italian boys stand close to their older brother—who clutches a picture of a saint—outside the main building on Ellis Island.

A CLOSER LOOK:
THE ROLE OF THE *PADRONE*

The *padrone* (boss) was supposed to function as an employment agent, travel agent, and sponsor. In reality, the *padroni* were free to swindle the ignorant immigrant, and they often did. Originally the *padrone* would go to Italy and recruit unemployed peasants, paying for their passage and providing jobs in the United States. The *padrone* often overcharged for these services, and did not provide suitable living quarters.

Most *padroni* took a fee from employers while also charging immigrants for finding jobs for them. They also overcharged for transportation to job sites (and anything else they could think of), and levied exorbitant interest rates on loans. Another insidious scheme of the *padroni* was to use the gullible peasants as strike-breakers, making the Italian immigrants even more hated by the workers they displaced.

The money-grabbing *padroni* were successful in fleecing immigrants because the foreigners could not speak English well enough to find a job for themselves, and the large cities where they usually landed were intimidating to the southern farmers. Some *padroni* were truly trying to help the immigrants, and despite its shortcomings the *padrone* system seems to have brought some short-term relief to the bewildered immigrants. At the turn of the century *padroni* controlled about two-thirds of the Italian laborers in New York, but soon enough the immigrants would be savvy enough to leave the *padrone* and attend to their own business.

(*Background*) "The Padrone." Sketch from scenes in "Mulberry Bend." Photo © Corbis-Bettmann.

FINDING THE WAY IN AMERICA

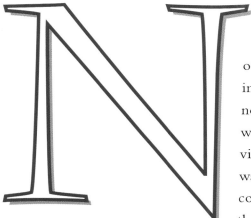

othing was familiar to the Italian immigrants in *lamerica*, and there was no way to transform the streets they walked on now into the roads of their villages in the *Mezzogiorno*. Not only was the language different, which of course they knew ahead of time, but there were so many things they hadn't expected—why, there were not even any numerals on American coins! From the very start, so much was so strange.

Since American cities were growing rapidly, most Italian immigrants settled in urban areas close to the places where unskilled labor was needed, and found jobs where speaking English was not required. They worked in construction, as ditchdiggers, hod carriers, and stonecutters. They built roads, dug tunnels for subways, laid cables and railroad tracks, and buried gas pipes under sidewalks—and they worked cheap.

Most early immigrants who set foot in New York City at the Battery in lower Manhattan just kept walking about thirty blocks uptown until they got to Mulberry Street, where thousands of other Italian immigrants had already settled in overcrowded slums filled with fire-trap tenements. This area of Mulberry Street, where the street turns abruptly into its own pri-

The alley of a slum dwelling at 24 Baxter Street in New York City. The scene shows the usual conflict between the generally unsanitary conditions of the streets and the ever-present clean laundry hanging from improvised clotheslines. These ramshackle houses in the Lower East Side were known as the "Dens of Death." The public-health inspector said in 1869, that these are "houses into which sunlight never enters.... It is no exaggeration to say that the money paid to the owners as rent is literally the 'price of blood'." Photo by Jacob Riis.

vate space, was known as "Mulberry Bend," the worst slum in New York City. (In 1901 Mulberry Bend was converted into Mulberry Park, and opened to the public.) Another favorite place was farther up, on West 22nd Street, a section known as "Hell's Kitchen." This was a tough neighborhood where each nation of immigrants had their own block, with little or no fraternization between them. Wherever the Italians settled, the streets were enlivened by the music of organ grinders, hurdy-gurdy players, amateur musicians, and the singsong calls of street peddlers.

The slums of London that Charles Dickens wrote about so eloquently in novels like *Oliver Twist* held about 175,000 people per square mile; the Lower East Side of New York City at the beginning of the twentieth century held almost 300,000 people per square mile. One block of tenements in Mulberry Bend might house 1,200 or more immigrants, perhaps ten to a room if the occupants were all male workers or all members of one family.

(Above) A combination bank and bar on the busy corner of Hester and Mulberry streets, 1893. It also served as an after-hours gathering place for neighborhood men.

(Following spread) Mulberry Street, New York City, c. 1900, the center of activity for so many Italian immigrants who came here directly from Ellis Island. At the extreme rear of the photograph the street curves back into the notorious Mulberry Bend, where strangers entered at their peril. Photo by Jacob Riis.

Ragpickers at rest in New York City, 1896. Early immigrants earned money any way they could, and ragpicking was a common pursuit. Old rags and clothes were usually sold to paper manufacturers for recycling. Baxter Street alley, shown earlier, was known as "Rag-picker's Row."

(In the Lower East Side during the peak periods of immigration there were more people living in that small area than in any city outside of Asia.)

There were better living conditions outside of Mulberry Bend, but even those places were overcrowded and overcharged. Greedy landlords were free to charge whatever they could get for their run-down coldwater flats, with the only heat coming from coal-burning stoves in the kitchen, where the family spent their waking hours. The immigrants had to buy their own coal, as well as their own ice for the icebox. Both commodities came from street peddlers, and the iceman was a special favorite of the children because if they were lucky they could get a small piece of ice to suck on. Naturally, the children did not notice that they were living in a slum, always having, or inventing, a street game to play, or a cranky street peddler to torment.

As small colonies of Italian immigrants called "Little Italys" sprang up in major American cities, Italians from different regions of Italy were often forced to learn to live together, a practice they had avoided in the old country. Italian immigrants adopted the American customs that were useful to them, yet held on to many of the old regional ways they were not yet ready to give up.

People who lived in Little Italys experienced more crowding than in established parts of the city. Fortunately, slum living was usually only temporary. Most immigrants left the worst ghettos like Mulberry Bend within a year, fanning out in all directions of the city to Greenwich Village, Hell's Kitchen on the west side, large areas of Harlem that became known as Italian Harlem, and the other boroughs of New York City. The completion of the Brooklyn Bridge in 1883, built in part with Italian labor, opened the way for the influx into Brooklyn; by 1935 two-thirds of the residents of south Brooklyn were Italian Americans. Some adventurous immigrants moved to faraway places like California, where social conditions were different from those in large eastern cities, and whose Little Italys were less crowded and less inclined to be slums.

FRANK LESLIE'S **ILLUSTRATED** NEWSPAPER

Entered according to Act of Congress, in the year 1883, by MRS. FRANK LESLIE, in the Office of the Librarian of Congress at Washington.— Entered at the Post Office, New York, N.Y., as Second-class Matter.

No. 1,440.—Vol. LVI }   NEW YORK—FOR THE WEEK ENDING APRIL 28, 1883.   [PRICE, 10 CENTS. $4.00 YEARLY. 13 WEEKS, $1.00

NEW YORK.—COMPLETING A GREAT WORK—LASHING THE STAYS OF THE BROOKLYN BRIDGE.
FROM A SKETCH BY A STAFF ARTIST.—SEE PAGE 153.

Completing the building of the Brooklyn Bridge, 1883. Many of the laborers were Italian. The new bridge was the main entry of immigrants into Brooklyn from Manhattan. Other bridges would soon follow as the need to travel from one borough to another increased rapidly.

A CLOSER LOOK:
PIECE WORK

Many Italian immigrants took work home from clothing factories to complete the garments. The activity was called "piece work" because the workers were paid by the piece. Men, women, and children took part, turning a tedious task into a group project that kept the family together at home, a crucial consideration for the family-oriented immigrants.

As the photo at right shows, the children even moved outdoors when possible. It was unusual for boys to crochet, but the nine-year-old boy on the far left had already been crocheting for two years when the photo was taken. Below, young Jennie Rizzandi works at home with her parents, New York City, c. 1912. Below right: bringing the piece work home was often a balancing act.

A makeshift jungle gym made of windows and fire escapes was enough to keep slum children playing happily. The basic resiliency of children provided opportunities for play everywhere. Even the debris on the ground would not have hampered an impromptu ballgame.

During the sweltering nights of July and August, fire escapes all over the Lower East Side, and in all other poor neighborhoods of New York and many other large cities such as Boston, Philadelphia, and Chicago, where immigrants had been attracted in search of work, became outdoor bedrooms. Sometimes an entire family would sleep on a fire escape, being awakened by the brilliant sunrise and the everyday sounds of the city streets coming to life.

Despite the typical hardships of arriving almost penniless in a new country, and the everyday discrimination leveled at new immigrants, Italians did adjust rather quickly, most of them having come from the rural areas of the *Mezzogiorno* and now having to live in the crowded city. Most immigrants got started in the slums of cities like New York, Philadelphia, Boston, and

Chicago, which were already overpopulated when they got there. The huge influx of more immigrants only added to the problem, at an alarmingly fast rate. Some newcomers died, especially the infants, helpless against hunger and new diseases that their tiny bodies had not yet learned to fight. At the end of the nineteenth century in Chicago, for example, 60 percent of the babies of immigrants died in their first year.

THE MIXED BLESSING OF *LA FAMIGLIA*

The foundation of the lives of Italian immigrants was the family (*la Famiglia*), which provided a core of dependability in an uncertain new environment. But as much as the family provided a real measure of security, it could also have a negative effect. For one thing, most Italian parents expected their children to stay close, even after they were married.

It was most likely family ties that brought this new immigrant to Vermont country.

Italian-speaking immigrants with children had a dilemma: Learn English as quickly as possible and speak only English in the house so that the children would be "Americanized" sooner. Or force the children to speak Italian at home so that the parents could always understand them, even if the children were speaking only English in order to avoid "being Italian"? Or speak Italian and English in the home so that the children would be bilingual? There was no set solution, but many parents took the easy way out and spoke only Italian.

Some Italian parents discouraged education also, not only because they did not understand the value of education in the United States, but also because they believed that education

An enterprising young boy sells his wares on Mulberry Street, while several idle men stand around hoping for better days. Street vendors dotted the urban areas of cities throughout the United States, as Italian immigrants resorted to familiar Old World customs to earn a living. The Italian bread sold outdoors was often a day or two old, and sold for less-than-bakery prices.

would drive their children away, supposedly instilling the idea that they were better than their parents. Although the family provided stability and a place to feel safe while the immigrants learned a new language and customs, such a backward attitude toward education sometimes placed restrictions on second-generation children, who did not want to be held back in a society that offered so many opportunities, and had to work that much harder to succeed. Even though many Italians did understand the value of education, some distrusted it and preferred their children to leave school as soon as it was possible for them to get a job and contribute to the family's livelihood.

Italian immigrants, like most immigrants, tended to live close together with relatives, or *paesani* (Italians who came from the same region of Italy in the long-standing tradition of *la Famiglia*). Within each Little Italy there might be even smaller units of *paesani*. New members of a group were helped by settled immigrants to get a job or find an inexpensive, relatively safe place where they could live and work.

THE SELF-SUFFICIENT SOUTHERNERS

Few Italians in America became public burdens. At the end of the nineteenth century less than 2 percent of the street beggars in New York City were Italian, while 8 percent were German, and 15 percent were Irish. In the same way, Italians chose not to seek help from institutions. In New York City in 1910 there were more than two thousand Italian Mutual Aid Societies, but typically, most Italian immigrants shied away from them. Italians expected family support rather than governmental aid—they distrusted organizations of any kind—and probably most important, most Italians preferred to work, no matter how menial the job, than to take charity.

The primary goal of the Italian immigrant was to earn a daily living for himself and his family. He was a hard worker who found little time for play or culture, usually working longer hours than immigrants of other nation-

A little girl about to enjoy a soft pretzel sold by a street vendor in New York City, c. 1909. Pretzels were often baked in sweltering basement bakeries and sold on the street for as little as two for a penny—and they were fresh!

A CLOSER LOOK:
THE LAWRENCE TEXTILE STRIKE

The Lawrence textile strike began on January 12, 1912, at the Lawrence mill in eastern Massachusetts. It was led by Italians and the leadership of the radical union, Industrial Workers of the World (IWW). Previously, Italian workers were involved in labor strikes only as "scabs," strikebreakers who would work for less than the workers who were on strike. Sometimes the Italians understood the implications of what they were doing, but usually they were merely following the instructions of *padroni,* unaware that the striking workers would resent the scabs, or even try to injure or kill them.

The background of the strike was this: The Lawrence textile mills, owned by the huge American Woolen Company, employed thirty thousand workers, about seven thousand of whom were Italian immigrants. Living conditions were among the poorest in the northeast, and salaries were low; a full fifty-six-hour week brought less than nine dollars. In order to survive, all members of a family had to work. When the Massachusetts legislature passed a law reducing the work week to fifty-four hours it seemed to be a blessing for the workers, however small, until the owners responded by cutting salaries proportionately. The seemingly small loss in pay was a major blow to the already underpaid workers.

A sudden mass confusion among the workers began, and the mills came to a halt as twenty thousand workers were suddenly on strike, marching and singing through the town. Lawrence officials

responded by activating about a thousand members of the militia, armed with artillery and machine guns. Their presence angered the strikers even further, and skirmishes broke out everywhere. On January 16 the troops drew their bayonets and charged the strikers. Several strikers were injured, and one boy was killed.

The clashes continued until the women took charge, sending over one hundred of their children to New York by train, where they were met at Grand Central Station by members of the Italian Socialist Federation. The New York press was shocked at the poor physical condition of the children—many of them had rickets caused by malnutrition—and sympathy quickly swung from the mill owners to the strikers. The public outrage in favor of the strikers reached a national level when twenty-five striking women in Lawrence, some pregnant, were arrested for child neglect. Now

in the midst of congressional hearings, the workers were close to a settlement. By the end of March 1912 the strike was over.

Perhaps the mill owners had the last laugh anyway. They speeded up their machines to increase productivity.

(Opposite) Striking textile workers face off against armed troops at the outset of the Lawrence textile strike in January 1912.

(Below) The strike was finally settled dramatically when the women of Lawrence decided to send children of the workers to New York City as a graphic protest of the harsh conditions imposed by management. The ploy worked when the highly publicized event produced nationwide outrage at the undernourished appearance of the children.

Ralph Fasanella. *The Great Strike*. 1978. Fasanella actually moved to Lawrence for three years before painting this picture, one of three versions he completed. With financial help from the Massachusetts Department of Environmental Management and private contributors, the city of Lawrence purchased one of Fasanella's strike paintings. It hangs in the Heritage State Park Visitor's Center, which was once a workers' boardinghouse near which the militia clashed with strikers in 1912. Courtesy of Eva Fasanella.

alities. If he couldn't find a job he sold rags or anything else he could find in the streets. The women and children did their part by taking home "piece work"—making lace doilies, for example—that the whole family could work on during any spare time they might have. Working at home was also valuable to the tradition of *la Famiglia* because it allowed the members of the family to be together while still earning money for honest work.

Politically, Italian immigrants came to America with certain issues that separated them from other immigrant groups. In their old country they were most recently oppressed by people of the same nationality and religion as their own, unlike the Irish, for example, who had had to contend with the Protestant English. As a result, the Italians knew they could not rely on

The imposing members of the St. Joseph Mutual Aid Society, Cincinnati, 1925. Earlier in the century many Italian Americans frequently shunned such groups, mistrusting organizations of any kind.

their political leaders, and instead formed a fierce attachment and loyalty to the family, believing that it was the only social institution on which they could depend. Fortunately, this attitude became less extreme as Italian Americans became more familiar with American ways, and at the start of the twenty-first century Italians have come to understand and make full use of social, political, and cultural institutions.

Ironically, one of the institutions the Italian Americans *did* approve of was closely connected to the government: civil service. Working for the city accomplished several things for the Italian American. It kept the family together in the same city, it provided steady work where the chances of being fired were slim except for the most serious offenses, and it rewarded hard work with regular promotions and pay raises, however slight that pay might be. Long-term municipal jobs were the Italian immigrants' idea of a safe career, not executive or other similar occupations that they thought were risky. Italians, for all of their verve in so many ways, taught their children that simple living without "showing off" was the only suitable way. In fact, if one Italian called another a "show-off" it was considered a very serious criticism, one that called for immediate self-improvement in that

Construction of the Empire State Building in the 1930s demanded nerves of steel while balancing on cables high above the busy city of New York. Many constrction workers were Italian immigrants. Photo by Lewis Hine.

A child outside a turn-of-the-century Italian family grocery store displaying many of the favorite foods—meats, cheeses, and dried fish among them. Photo © Corbis-Bettmann.

area. Italians were, and are, complex and fascinating people, and they have come a very long way.

FESTAS AND OTHER AMUSEMENTS

People in crisis always seem to find some relief. Despite the crowded and filthy tenements, Italian Americans found ways to light up the streets. Feasts and other amusements were almost a daily fare. A favorite festival in the Mulberry district honored Saint Rocco, revered among southern Italians for his miraculous cures of the diseased and maimed. Paraders reminded spectators of Saint Rocco's miracles by carrying wax arms, legs, hands, and other parts of the body. San Gennaro, the patron saint of Naples, was a huge favorite, and even today the Feast of San Gennaro in New York's Little Italy draws crowds from all over the tristate area, and, as with all the larger feasts, one need not be Catholic to have a wonderful time. The food alone guarantees that.

The immigrants from Palermo honored their patron saint, Santa Rosalia, who rescued Palermo from pestilence. Two other large festivals were held in the New York area every year. San Gandolfo, the patron saint of Polizzi Generoso, Sicily, was honored with a three-day event that included band concerts and singers, and ended with a parade followed by a grand procession for compatriots and the faithful. The culminating event of the procession was a "flight of angels," which was achieved by suspending two young girls dressed as angels on ropes stretched across a street between two fire escapes.

In Italy, the truly communal entertainment was the religious festival in honor of the Madonna. In New York, the annual celebration of the Madonna of Mount Carmel attracted worshippers from other cities and states, and her devotees often brought gold and silver plaques in gratitude for favors received. A float bearing a large statue of the Madonna was surrounded by schoolgirls and young women dressed in white, and was pulled

Studio family portraits were a must, no matter how hard the family had to scrimp to save enough money. Costumes were formal and elaborate. The fruits of marriage were dutifully recorded with formal studio portraits of the family. Props such as the pony and American flag in these photos were supplied by the studio. The occasions were meant to document the family growth and were therefore very serious.

(Right) Large Italian weddings seemed natural for such a family-oriented group. The occasion was thoughtful and formal. This 1927 union in Cincinnati, Ohio, presents a respectful celebration.

(Far right, top and bottom) A child's first Holy Communion was a solemn ritual that was honored by every Italian Catholic family with expensive "pure" white outfits for girls and boys, and the usual studio photograph complete with props. Probably nowhere was the Italian family tie to the Church more evident than in the observance of first Holy Communion.

(Above) No less serious
an occasion, but more
obviously joyful than the
earlier wedding, these
young women look
ready to celebrate.

(Right) Gracefully
acknowledging the
poignancy of the
moment, this groom,
waiting at the altar,
accepts the hand of his
bride from her father.

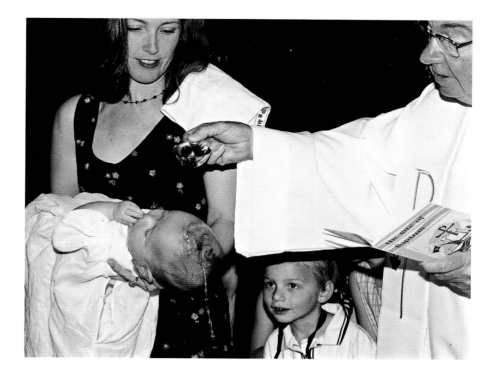

(Right and below) These photographs, taken in the 1990s, continue the tradition of family portraits and a ritual observance of baptism, but in a much more informal atmosphere than earlier in the century. Note the youngster checking to make sure the holy water actually touches the baby's head.

(*Above*) **A choir at an Italian street festival in New York City surrounds a statue of Mary and Jesus.**

(*Opposite*) **The Italian street festival of** *Il Giglio*. **The climax of the festivities, shown here, was the lifting of a seventy-foot tower, topped by a statue of St. Anthony. More than one hundred men carried the huge tower while onlookers observed from their decorated windows, fire escapes, and roofs to join in the fun. Photo © Daily Mirror/Corbis-Bettmann.**

through the streets of Italian East Harlem, with thousands of marchers behind it. The sight of the Madonna was enough to set off an explosion of fireworks and shouts from the spectators.

Next in popularity to the feast was the wedding ritual, beginning with the bridal party traveling in an open carriage from the bride's tenement to the church, with relatives and friends following on foot or in carriages. Outside the church after the ceremony, the bride and groom were gently but enthusiastically pelted with confetti and sugar-coated almonds—symbols of fertility—by the cheering throng. Wedding celebrations included the guests' children, and always brought back happy memories of weddings in the *Mezzogiorno*.

Festivals and weddings were not the only amusements for the children. In anticipation of Election Day celebrations—still weeks away—young boys stole straw hats from the heads of well-dressed men and strung them on a line between fire escapes. Hats were added to the string for months after-

(Above) Mother Cabrini (1850–1917), founder of the Congregation of the Missionary Sisters of the Sacred Heart, organized schools, hospitals, and homes for destitute Italian immigrants and their children. The first American citizen to become a saint, she was especially revered as the Saint of Immigrants. Because of her pioneering efforts, teaching orders like the Jesuits and Franciscans began to provide bilingual teachers for their Catholic schools in Italian neighborhoods. Photo © Bettmann/ CORBIS.

(Opposite) Maria Bonfanti, of the renowned Bonfanti Ballet Troupe, in *The Black Crook.*

ward, until a necklace of fancy hats stretched across the street. All this time, old furniture was collected and hidden away. The furniture was brought out after dark one night by boys "from sixteen to seventy," and piled high in the street underneath the hats. Then, as everyone in the streets and in windows cheered, the pile of furniture was lighted, with the idea of setting the hats on fire. Some people shrieked as they saw their "missing" furniture go up in joyous flames.

Besides feasts, wedding ceremonies, and election parties, the early immigrants in New York found their *divertimenti* close to home in vaudeville and the theater, puppet shows, musical performances, picnics, and family games. At most of the larger gatherings there was music—Italian arias and songs from a gramophone or a player-piano pumped with gusto by one of the children. There were theater clubs set up in hired halls and cafes. A typical evening in one of the Bowery's hired halls included farces in Sicilian or Neapolitan dialect. Comedies such as *Pasca' si a'nu porcu* ("Pascal, You're a Pig") were followed by a grand ball and entertainment by mandolin soloists, singers, and even prizefighters. Some of the theaters presented serious drama, but the actors always had competition from the audience, which would become as talkative as if they were at a wedding or a picnic.

The satirical singer Farfariello ("Little Butterfly") arrived in the United States from Naples in 1898, and soon became the idol of the Italian community. His real name was Edoardo Migliaccio. Bored with work in the needle trades he began to appear in cafes singing Neapolitan songs. In his sketches, Farfariello portrayed a fast-talking, quick-witted greenhorn with his own set of cultural values, thus turning the tables on the ethnic stereotype. The immigrants saw themselves in Farfariello's comedy, and they

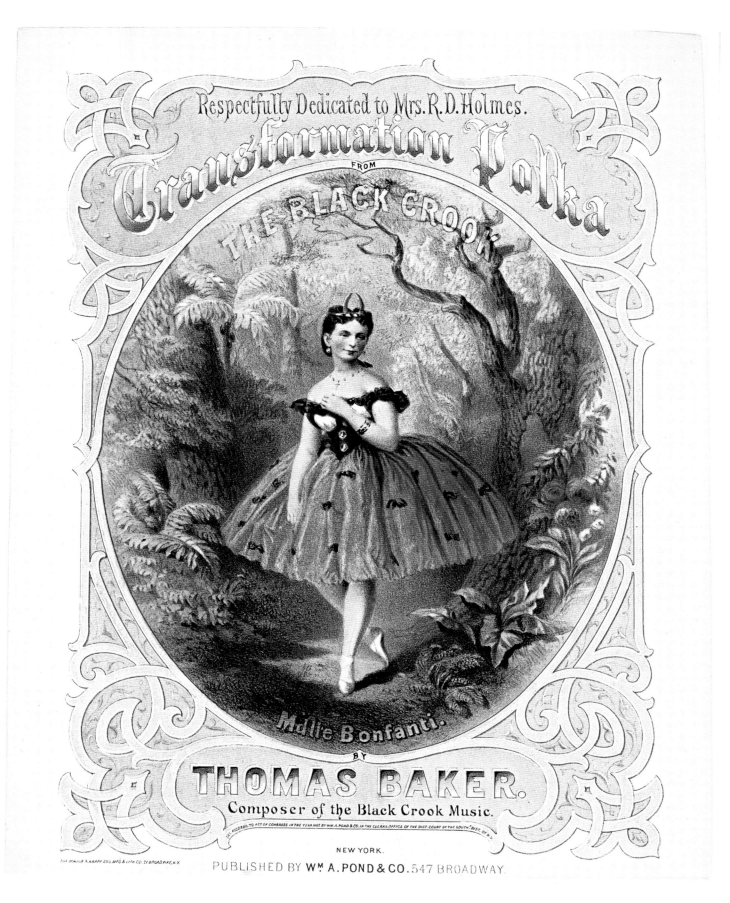

loved him. Farfariello's popularity became a significant factor in the establishment of San Francisco's Washington Square Theater, where he was invited to perform. The theater, whose admission charge was ten cents for plays and opera, became a center for the Italian community.

Edoardo Migliaccio, "Farfariello," c. 1910.

Italian-American theater prospered through the 1920s. Farfariello used his native Neapolitan in his acts, but he attracted Italians from other regions. as did the Sicilian immigrant Giovanni DiRosalia, whose character "Norfio" attracted large audiences of Italians from all over the *Mezzogiorno*. Immigrants who could not afford the opera went to the *Opera dei Puppi*, puppet shows whose mainstay was the battle between Christian knights and Saracen warriors. The most noted practitioner of Sicilian puppetry was Agrippino Manteo, who emigrated here in 1919.

A.W. Millard, Jr. *The Great Costello*. The Barnum Museum. A banner advertising James Costello, early-twentieth century magician and illusionist, who performed with Ringling Bros. and Barnum & Bailey Circus. His dancing-on-glass routine was a featured attraction at the circus sideshow.

T. Wharf.
Boston.

EXTENDING THE BOUNDARIES

Except for the "birds of passage" who moved from town to town as jobs arose, then home again, Italians in Italy were happy to stay put in the towns and villages they called home. So it is interesting that there was mobility among the Italian immigrants in the United States. They went wherever they needed to go to find work, to support their families.

(Opposite) **Merchants and dock workers crowd Boston's Fisherman's Wharf, c. 1890. Boston was a popular settling place for Italian immigrants.**

The first wave of immigrants reached its peak in 1854, with over four hundred thousand people leaving their home countries. The second wave of ten million came from 1865 to the 1880s. These two early waves were the "old" (basically non-Italian) immigrants, consisting of people from Ireland, Germany, and other countries in northern and western Europe; they arrived in the United States between 1815 and the 1880s.

The "old" immigrants were followed by the "new" immigrants from southern and eastern Europe. About seventeen million "new" immigrants came to the United States from about 1880 to 1914, when World War I started. Contained within that seventeen million were over four million Italians, mostly from the south.

Many Italians in the "new" wave of immigrants landed in New York City, but many also kept traveling on to other cities. About 75 percent went to

Sardines. at Eastport Me

Sardines are laid out neatly to dry on the dock at Eastport, Maine, c. 1900. Many Italian immigrants flocked to the famil-iarity of fishing ports all across the country.

cities in upstate New York, Pennsylvania, Massachusetts, and New Jersey. Others settled in New England, or Illinois and Ohio, attracted by job opportunities in Chicago and Cleveland, and some brave souls crossed the country to seek their fortunes in Washington, Oregon, Colorado, and California. New Jersey attracted many immigrants, as did Connecticut and other New England states. Others went to Philadelphia, Baltimore, Boston, and practically every other city in the United States.

San Francisco was the favorite destination on the west coast. (In the 1880s, steerage passage from the east to California cost forty dollars. By the turn of the century transcontinental railroads had shortened the coast-to-coast journey from five months to five days.) California came to be called the "Italy of America" because of its climate and geography. The opportunity for immigrants to own their own small businesses was much greater in California than in the eastern and midwestern cities, and immigrants who traveled to California usually stayed there, eventually owning orchards, dairies, truck farms, and fishing businesses.

Italian immigrants may have been farmers in the *Mezzogiorno*, but most of them chose to give up the idea of returning to the land in favor of the more likely possibility of economic security in large cities. They had seen enough of the vagaries of farming. Now they wanted security, which they believed they would obtain in the cities, although several successful communities existed in western states, where small-scale truck farms did not have to be owned by the farmers, and other operations such as selling cut flowers, winemaking, fishing, and fruit and vegetable canning were offering good opportunities.

The Italian-American writer Pasquale d'Angelo noted that "on the farms [the Italians] showed what hard work and intensive cultivation could do to make abandoned farms bloom. They proved that supposedly worthless land, sandy or pine brush, could be reclaimed."

In 1910, Italian immigrants were living in the following large cities in the United States: New York: 340,765 (67 percent); Philadelphia: 45,308 (9 per-

(Opposite) **A Sicilian tenant farmer demonstrates for young Sophy, the landowner's granddaughter, the fine details of shelling fava beans. Photo by Diane Hamilton.**

cent); Chicago: 45,169 (9 percent); Boston: 31,380 (6 percent); San Francisco: 16,918 (3 percent); Pittsburgh: 14,120 (3 percent); New Orleans: 8066 (2 percent); and Baltimore: 5,043 (1 percent). At that same time, there were more Italians living in New York City than in Florence, Venice, and Genoa combined, with most of the Italian immigrants in New York City living in Manhattan and Brooklyn.

The great majority of Italian Americans settled in cities. By the middle of the twentieth century, Waterbury, Connecticut, had the highest proportion of Italian Americans, who comprised 23 percent of its total population. Waterbury was followed by New Haven, Connecticut (22 percent of its population), Paterson, New Jersey (20 percent), Providence, Rhode Island (19 percent), Newark, New Jersey, and Rochester, New York (each 16 percent), Somerville, Massachusetts (15 percent), and Trenton, New Jersey (14 percent). New York City had 13 percent Italian-American residents, Boston had 10 percent, and San Francisco had 7 percent.

PHILADELPHIA

Italians were living in Philadelphia before the Revolutionary War, but it was not until the 1850s that one could speak of an Italian community there. As early as 1853, an Italian community had established the first Italian national parish in the United States. Most of these first settlers were artists and musicians who had lived near Genoa. By 1900, Italians were the largest foreign-born group in Philadelphia, with forty-five thousand inhabitants, and Philadelphia had the second-largest community of Italian Americans after New York City.

Much of the early history of Italians in Philadelphia revolves around six Italian-American families, but the career of Frank DiBerardino may be the most representative. DiBerardino came to the United States from Abruzzo, and in 1887 he established the DiBerardino Bank and a steamship ticket agency. He also furnished the Pennsylvania Railroad with laborers by paying the passage of immigrants from his native Abruzzo. A *padrone* in the best sense, DiBerardino charged no interest on his loans, and he brought

"Breaker Boys" working in the Ewen Breaker mine, South Pittston, Pennsylvania, 1911. Children were often favored as mine workers because their small size allowed them to work in the cramped mine shafts more comfortably than grown men. Photo by Lewis Hine.

thirty-seven thousand immigrants from all over Italy to the United States from 1900 to 1940, establishing work camps from Pennsylvania to North Carolina. He met the immigrant ships in person.

By 1910 a new Italian community had come into being in South Philadelphia, extending its boundaries all the way to the Delaware River.

BALTIMORE

In 1874 there were about forty Italian ships in Baltimore harbor, most of which took part in the triangular trade that brought Italian marble and luxury items from Italy, picked up grain in Baltimore for England, and there loaded coal for the furnaces of northern Italy. The first immigrants to settle in Baltimore were from Genoa, the home port of this trade route. When Italians first arrived in Baltimore they found a city that was both

A group of forlorn children in a Boston back alley. Compare these children with those seen opposite.

Young berry-pickers have escaped the Philadelphia heat for the wilds of Delaware, c. 1910. Note the cocky boy in front smoking a cigarette. The summer sun and fresh air could only have a good effect on the health of these children even though many worked long hours collecting buckets of berries. Photo by Lewis Hine.

southern and German. The German population was so large, in fact, that the city's laws had to be published in German.

Most of the first Italian residents of Baltimore were sculptors or in some other way associated with marble monuments, but by 1903 common laborers began to arrive, finding work at a dollar a day. As usual, these workers formed Little Italys close to their work sites. Eight mutual aid societies had a total membership of about a thousand immigrants, mostly from southern Italy, and the Italian conclave became tightly knit, establishing their political power by electing the first Italian representative from Baltimore, Vincent Palmisano, a native of Termini, Sicily.

BOSTON

The first small enclave of Italians in Boston were mostly Genovesi, who settled in the 1860s. By 1875 Boston was the second largest port of entry for immigrants, behind New York, with an influx of Sicilians, Abruzzese, and Neapolitans in the 1890s that raised the population of the North End to over seven thousand.

A family-owned and operated Italian grocery store in Chicago, 1928. Similar establishments still exist throughout the United States, offering food lovers of all nationalities a cornucopia of authentic Italian treats. If you wanted it so, Italy was never far away.

The Sicilians were the most recent arrivals, and they filled the entire length of North Street, near the fishing piers. Many of the Sicilians had come from fishing villages on the Sicilian coast, and made good use of Boston's fishing facilities. Some Sicilians moved instead to smaller coastal cities of Massachusetts, such as Gloucester or Rockport, where they shared the fishing waters with the Portuguese.

By the turn of the century the Italians had supplanted the Irish as the largest immigrant group in Boston, and tenements in the North End were

occupied primarily by people from Campania, Sicily, and Genoa. Because of the earlier misuse of the section by the Irish and Germans, and the increasingly dense population of Italians, the North End had become Boston's first slum.

It was from this shaky foothold in Boston that thousands of immigrants went to work in the textile mills of Lawrence, Massachusetts, the site of the devastating labor strike in 1912.

CHICAGO

Between 1890 and 1910, Chicago's population gained a million people, making the total population 2,185,283. Chicago became the second-largest city behind New York, and housing became a serious problem.

Most of the Italian enclaves were in the city's vice district called Little Hell, and Chicago had become known as the most wicked city in the United States, especially the Cicero section, which would later become the territory of Al Capone. Little Hell was crowded with gin mills, whore-

An upscale barbershop in Chicago, in 1916, run by Italian immigrants who were probably barbers in Italy before they emigrated to the United States.

Italian crane operators working on the Grand Trunk Railroad in Chicago, c. 1929.

houses, gambling joints, and other disreputable operations. The police stayed clear. Poverty and organized crime had preceded the Italians in Little Hell, which was previously occupied by Swedes and Irish. When these two groups moved on, Little Hell became known as "Little Sicily."

In the early days of immigration there was a strong sense of regionalism among the Italians. The Calabrese clustered around the Near West Side, while those from Potenza settled in Armour Square. Each church had to have an altar dedicated to the patron saint of a particular region; Saint Alessandro for the Calabrese, The Virgin of the Rosary for the Sicilians. Friction between the relatively wealthy Genovesi (who had been the first to come) and immigrants from the *Mezzogiorno* was intense, and in fact, competition among immigrants from all different regions was openly strong.

The newspapers in Chicago exaggerated southern Italian stereotypes by depicting the southerner—especially the Sicilians—as knife-wielding hotheads. This image was not helped by the presence of enslaved Italian children who roamed the streets in gangs, begging in the guise of strolling musicians. The children had been brought into Chicago by unscrupulous *padroni* after a police crackdown in New York forced them westward.

Between 1871 and 1890 the mastermind behind much of the crime in Chicago was not an Italian, but an Irishman, one Michael Cassius McDonald. Anyone who wanted to operate within the red-light district had to "see Mike," arranging to pay over a large proportion of their profits to him. Although McDonald never held an elected office, he ruled the city, and chose the politicians who would be nominated, elected, and then become his puppets.

Until 1914 Little Sicily remained a tight little island, almost a replica of a Sicilian village, isolated by poor transportation and hemmed in by the sounds of the booming city. Because jobs were so hard to find, even skilled workers settled for unskilled jobs on the railroad tracks or on construction projects. Tailors, barbers, and shoemakers were able to follow their old

The Wagon Road Bridge in Cincinnati, built mainly by Italian immigrants, was constructed to accommodate the Cincinnati Railroad, 1870.

Stone carvers at work
on the monumental
sculpture for the
fourth Wisconsin
State Capitol building,
c. 1912.

trades, but most Italians were happy to provide the pick-and-shovel labor needed to maintain the two thousand miles of track within the city limits. But with the onset of World War I there was a great shortage of labor, and Italians were finally able to secure higher-paying jobs that were previously closed to them. Not only were the workers receiving more money, they became integrated with other ethnic groups from whom they had been isolated. Even women found work in the garment industry.

By the turn of the century Italians had organized a Socialist Party, which fostered a number of union organizers such as Emilio Grandinetti, who founded the Italian-language newspaper *Il Corriere Di Chicago* (The Chicago Courier), which became the guiding light for socialists and many of the strikers in the garment industry between 1910 and 1915. By 1919 over twenty-five thousand were members of the clothing workers union, and as a result both wages and living conditions were improved. Grandinetti eventually broke with the International Workers of the World (IWW) because its leaders would not work with Jews in the garment industry. Italian workers, eager to improve themselves, now took part in the growing labor struggles of their new country.

THE SOUTH

Soon after the Civil War, when the migration of ex-slaves to the north created a labor shortage in the south, Louisiana was one of the first southern states to encourage Italian immigration, with advertisements at Ellis Island and throughout southern Italy describing Louisiana as a land with a Mediterranean climate and plenty of jobs. By 1900 more than twenty-five hundred Italian immigrants arrived in Louisiana, most of them from Sicily. Some found jobs in the port of New Orleans, but most were recruited to work in the sugarcane fields, where they were supervised by armed guards and lived in worse conditions than those they had left behind.

Unskilled sugarcane workers toiled from sunup to sundown, often for no more than a dollar a day. In Sicily the sight of a woman working in the fields was rare, but now they joined their men in the fields. Old men, women, and boys were paid twenty-five or fifty cents a day. With the whole family working they could think about buying their own land, and an impressive number of immigrants working in the south were able to do just that.

Some immigrants in Louisiana freed themselves from being overworked and underpaid by chipping in to buy a small piece of land near the town of Independence. They succeeded in organizing a model agricultural community with the cultivation of just one crop—strawberries. Many of these farmers were able to send for their families in Palermo, triggering an emigration that continued for generations.

Many Italian immigrants found their way to Texas and other southern states, where they sometimes learned that it was better to join together than to try to live apart from the support of other Italian immigrants.

The more enterprising immigrants moved westward to Texas, where they worked as section hands on the railroads being built there. When those jobs ended the workers moved to towns such as Hearne, Caldwell, and Dilly Shaw to work as sharecroppers until they could save enough money to buy their own land. Others sought jobs in the oilfields of Dickenson or Galveston. The Texas farming town that drew the most Sicilians (about twenty-four hundred from Poggioreale, Corleone, and Salaparuta) was Bryan, in Brazos County. The immigrants pooled their money and bought land, which they cleared and planted with cotton and corn for sale, and other vegetables for themselves. It was not an easy life, and the worst times came in 1899 and 1900, when the Brazos river overflowed. Thirty-five people were killed, and property damage was estimated at $9 million. The ancient Sicilian proverb, "The man who plays alone never loses," was put aside as mutual trust became the Sicilians' major defense against failure.

THE WEST

Italian immigrants generally fared better in the west, where the population consisted largely of newcomers who were more tolerant of foreigners. An exception was Colorado, where the Italians came, along with Slovaks, Poles, and Russians, to work in the mining camps. The presence of so many foreign workers angered the English-speaking workers who were already there, and the employers took advantage of the Italian workers' ignorance of the new country. The workers' only defense seemed to be the formation of labor unions, and when they went on strike they were defeated and forced to leave the area. Five years later, the governor of Colorado declared martial law to put down a union strike at Cripple Creek, and shootings and lynching were not uncommon in the tough mining towns. And yet, by 1910 about forty thousand Italian Americans were living in Colorado, with many settling in Denver.

Italian immigrants in Arizona worked in the mines and on the extension of the Southern Pacific and Sante Fe railroads. But the Wild-West atmosphere of Arizona at that time was not agreeable to Italian family life. In 1910 there were only about fifteen hundred Italians living in Arizona, and that number declined soon after.

In Wyoming, the most sparsely settled of all the states, the Italians worked as miners and railroad workers. Some became farmers or sheep ranchers. Only a handful of Italians came to Nevada or the state of Washington, and those that did come to Washington were drawn by Seattle. The Italians had been encouraged to travel to Seattle by reports of a lush Pacific seaport and plenty of work. Seattle was indeed growing rapidly, and Italian laborers joined the Scandinavians, Germans, and Japanese who were already working there. Between 1900 and 1910 the population of Seattle tripled from

Italian miners in the Bunker Hill mine in Coeur d'Alene, Idaho. Italian Americans went where the work was, even all the way out to Idaho.

80,000 to 240,000, but the Italian population remained relatively small, probably because the Italians, next to the Japanese, were considered the least desirable foreign group.

COMMUNITY FARMING IN THE NEW WORLD

Although the majority of Italian immigrants came from farmlands—from 1891 to 1910 almost 500,000 Italian immigrants had been farmers—relatively few continued to farm in the United States. This was partially because they could not afford to buy land, and also because the isolated nature of farming in America did not appeal to them. The Italian peasant farmer was used to working in the fields during the day and enjoying the social life of the village in the evening. The loneliness of American farm life was seen as an invitation to illness.

Truck farmers packing newly picked fruit. More women than men and children pitched in here, but everyone shared the job, and apparently enjoyed the country air.

Tomato-harvest time
in the incredibly
successful Italian
farming community
of Vineland, New
Jersey, c. 1915.

But even in the cities, the love of farming transformed itself in a modest way. Wherever there were backyards the Italians found a little patch of land where they could grow the same vegetables they had grown in Italy. The tiny backyard sometimes included a small grape vine or a fig tree, which was nurtured by warm summers and wrapped in rags during the winter. Where there were no backyards, as in most places in Manhattan, the Italians found land in the Bay 50th area near Brooklyn's Coney Island. Many of these small plots fed the burgeoning truck-farming industry, whose fresh produce was sold from pushcarts by street peddlers.

Truck farming was attractive to Italian immigrants for several reasons. They could pursue it in their spare time, they did not need the usual array of heavy farm tools, the whole family could help, and it kept alive the familiar atmosphere of working with friends and family. By the 1920s Italians were recognized as the country's chief suppliers of fresh fruits and vegetables. Their success in truck farming encouraged some immigrants to find a place outside the city where they could grow their produce, while still

A CLOSER LOOK:
THE CITY BY THE BAY

Tony Bennett (Benedetto) may have been raised in Queens, New York, but he left his heart in San Francisco. A lot of other Italian Americans did too. The image of American streets paved with gold may have struck Italians for the first time in 1848, when gold was discovered near San Francisco, the city named by Spaniards to honor one of Italy's favorite saints, Saint Francis. Among those hit with gold fever were several hundred Italians from northern Italy. Even Italian sailors on ships bringing Carrara marble to San Francisco jumped ship to go searching for gold.

But most Italians arrived too late to stake out claims, and went on to settle in the fertile Sacramento–San Joaquin Valley, or traveled north to Oregon and Washington. Those immigrants that remained opened restaurants, groceries, and clothing stores. By 1870 there were only about sixteen hundred Italians in San Francisco, but fifty years later they were the leading immigrant group, making up 20 percent of all foreign-born residents.

The Italians first settled around Telegraph Hill, a rocky bluff that

stretched down to the waterfront. The Italians started at the bottom of the Hill, with Irish at the top and Germans in the middle, but as more Italians arrived they displaced the Irish and Germans, and then also moved into the North Beach section adjacent to Telegraph Hill. The combined section became known first as the Latin Quarter, and then as the Italian Quarter. At first the residents of the Italian Quarter were mostly fishermen and farmers, but twentieth-century arrivals from Italy included artisans, mechanics, shopkeepers, and restaurateurs. Some other farmers, mostly from Naples and Tuscany, who were determined to keep on farming, gravitated to the Outer Mission district, where they worked together to turn sandy dunes into productive farmland that was perfect for the production of lettuce and artichokes.

The Italians on Telegraph Hill saved the area from complete disaster during the 1906 earthquake. When fires began to creep up the Hill, the Italians rolled barrels of wine from their cellars and, forming a bucket brigade, they were able to protect their houses from the flames with blankets soaked in homemade wine.

By 1920, Italians made up 20 percent of all foreign-born residents in San Francisco, second only to New York City. Ten years later it was noted that 54 percent of the Italians in San Francisco were from northern Italy, 36 percent were from southern Italy, and 10 percent were from central Italy. The first Italian immigrants who came to San Francisco were from northern Italy, and they typically had more job skills than southern Italians. They also became active in banking and small industry, and took advantage of the wonderful fishing opportunities in the San Francisco area.

In fact, commercial fishing was San Francisco's second-most important industry behind truck farming. By 1910 Italian-American fishermen were doing most of the commercial fishing in California, and providing almost all of the fish that was consumed in San Francisco or shipped out of the state. The local economy was booming. Indeed, Italian Americans (as well as the Italian government) thought that the Italian-American community in San Francisco was the "model colony" in the United States, and that the immigrants themselves were the "most select" and desirable of any urban Italian Americans.

Fisherman's Wharf, which has since become famous as a tourist attraction, served as the harbor for seven hundred fishing vessels, which averaged a daily catch of 11,500 tons. The Genovesi were the first Italians to dominate the fishing industry in San Francisco, having driven off the Greeks and Slovaks. As a result of fierce competition with the Genovesi, groups of Sicilian fishermen left San Francisco to join *paesani* who were established in Monterey and Black Diamond (later called Pittsburg). The Sicilians were so successful that they were able to bring their families to the United States, increasing the population of Black Diamond to three thousand, all of them from *Isola delle Femmine*, an island off the coast of Sicily.

Other major businesses founded and operated by Italian-American immigrants included the Italian Swiss Colony Wine Company, the Del Monte Corporation, the Gallo Wine Company, and the Bank of Italy (later renamed the Bank of America). But credit for the success of San Francisco must go to all the Italian Americans who lived and worked there and in the surrounding Bay area. They, as much as bankers or vintners, helped San Francisco grow and prosper to become the special place it is.

(Above) **Retired men playing the Italian ever-favorite game of *bocci* at the special courts in Aquatic Park, San Francisco. Photo © Ted Streshinsky/CORBIS.**

(Opposite) **A group of fishermen of Italian descent prepare their bait and repair fishing gear, traps, and nets at Fisherman's Wharf in San Francisco, c. 1940.**

being close enough to the city to market it there. Farming communities began to spring up like backyard lettuce. A typical community was in Canastota, New York, between Utica and Syracuse. Canastota was surrounded by extensive tracts of mucklands, many of them undeveloped. The Italians cleared the swamplands and converted them into arable acres of farmland. Despite many difficulties, the Italians became the dominant onion growers in Canastota, and were credited as putting the community on the map, as "Onion Town."

Italians began settling in Vineland, New Jersey, as early as 1880. By 1910 about 950 families had turned it into the most successful farming colony in the United States. Vineland was established in the 1860s by Charles K. Landis, when it was a sprawling 57,000 acres of wilderness. He had a vision of happy homes surrounded by farms and gardens, and by offering uncleared land at twenty-five cents an acre, he succeeded in attracting nine thousand farmers within five years.

Landis had joined forces with Franceso Secchi de Casale, the editor of *L'Eco d'Italia*, to attract immigrants away from the cities. By 1880 there were about one hundred Italian families in Vineland, and in 1885 a new tract of land became known as "New Italy," with streets named after Italian provinces. The farmers were proudly (and profitably) introducing little-known Italian vegetables such as peppers, zucchini (squash), eggplant, fennel, and broccoli into the American marketplace. It is notable that not once did Landis have to institute foreclosure proceedings on any of the Italians in Vineland.

Other successful agricultural colonies were formed in Fredonia, New York; Genoa, Wisconsin; and Sunnyside and Tontitown, Arkansas.

**Thousands of Italian Americans gather in St. Paul, Minnesota, on October 12, 1931, to celebrate
the dedication of a statue of Columbus on the state capitol grounds.**

A CLOSER LOOK:
FUTURE ENTREPRENEURS?

Boys will be boys: Italian-American young boys all did their part to contribute to the family upkeep. Working was an activity for all—city slickers and small-town boys alike—from a very young age. These young "newsies" all project a jaunty style. The pensive, muscular mill worker lives in a different world.

(Left) After peddling their papers in a Syracuse, New York, saloon, these cocky newsies pose for a photograph with two saloon patrons who insisted on joining them.

(Below) Selling newspapers in front of the U.S. Capitol in Washington, D.C.

(Above) Newsies at
a busy trolley junction
in Jersey City, New
Jersey, 1912. Photo
by Lewis Hine.

(Left) A mill boy with
a totally different
kind of life than the
newsies. Note the
tattered clothing, and
muscular arms.

BATTLING DISCRIMINATION IN THE PROMISED LAND

Like all immigrant groups the Italians had to deal with discrimination, but time and again they overcame it, showing a resiliency and adaptability that helped them assimilate faster than any sociologist could have predicted. But there were seveal real obstacles; some were political, and some were violent.

Unlike other immigrant groups, Italian Americans kept silent when newspapers reported about them inaccurately. This attitude was a carryover from their impotent political position in Italy. Also, Italian Americans stayed within very small social circles, and had no interest in mixing with people in high places. In fact, Italian Americans distrusted all social, political, and cultural contacts, an old Italian tradition called *campanalismo*: Anything beyond the sound of the *campanile* (parish belltower) was not to be trusted. This was probably one of the most difficult self-defeating practices Italian Americans had to overcome.

The newly arrived Italians were despised most of all by the Irish, who preceded them into the United States. Naturally, immigrants who had been here a while looked down on all future immigrants, and the Irish had the Italians to kick around. Although both groups were usually Catholic, and may have even attended the same church, the Irish condemned what they perceived as the Italians' superstitions, religious feasts, saint-worship, and

(Opposite) **Ben Shahn (1898–1969).** *The Passion of Sacco and Vanzetti.* **1931–1932. Oil on tempera. Whitney Museum of American Art, New York. The painting, one of a series on the case of Sacco and Vanzetti, shows the Lowell Committee standing over the caskets of Sacco and Vanzetti (with mustache), with the Dedham County courthouse in the background, and the presiding Judge Thayer appearing in a window. © Estate of Ben Shahn/Licensed by VAGA, New York, NY.**

what seemed like statue-worship. But most of all, the Irish resented the Italians for taking many of their jobs away by working cheaper, or by acting as strikebreakers.

Whatever social and economic obstacles the Irish placed before the Italians, they were the least of the Italians' worries, compared to political obstacles, which came steadily. Between 1882 and 1913 the United States government imposed a head tax on arriving immigrants, prohibited the importation of contract labor, passed an act that gave the federal government the power to severely restrict foreign immigration for medical and other reasons, and in 1892 enacted the Quarantine Act, which gave the president the authority to prohibit all immigration in case of a foreign epidemic.

In 1886, at almost the same time that the Statue of Liberty was unveiled in New York Harbor, Iowans created the powerful anti-foreign, anti-Catholic American Protective Association, whose membership reached its peak in 1892, and in 1893 the Immigration Restriction League was formed in Boston. Apparently, not all of Europe's "huddled masses" were welcome in the United States, and the southern Italians were the current target of fervent nationalists.

Stimulated by earlier prodding from Senator Henry Cabot Lodge of Massachusetts, the United States Congress passed the Literacy Test Act in 1897, which would ban any immigrant over sixteen who could not read or write. Fortunately, since many southern Italians were illiterate, President Grover Cleveland vetoed the bill, but high-level discrimination continued. In 1902 future president Woodrow Wilson wrote that southern Italian immigrants came from the "lowest class" of Italians, having neither skill nor intelligence.

In 1913 President William H. Taft vetoed another attempt by Congress to pass a bill requiring a literacy test for immigrants, stating that immigrants had been denied the opportunity to obtain an education in Europe, and should not be penalized for seeking that opportunity in the United States.

A feature in *Harper's Weekly* about the New Italian School on Leonard Street in New York City, 1875. The school was built for the moral and mental improvement of the Italian population. Here we see band practice and sewing and embroidery classes. For several years the school was closed by decision of the Roman Catholic priests who worked on the superstitious fears of the Italians and made them believe that the real objective of the school was to draw them away from their religion. But the students persisted, and the older students even formed associations for further study, music being a high priority. All this while many of the students were holding jobs in shops and factories. *Harper's* stated, "Their assiduity, attention, and perseverance have elicited the admiration of all their friends," and enlisted the participation of individuals who add financial support.

A CLOSER LOOK:
DAGO, GUINEA, WOP: WHAT DO THEY MEAN?

As any Italian American knows, the slang words *dago*, *guinea*, and *wop* are all derogatory terms given to Italian immigrants, and they persist to a lesser degree even today. There are several ideas about the origins of these three offensive words, and we will start with the accounts in Webster's Third New International Dictionary. According to Webster's, *dago* was derived from the Spanish word for James, *Diego*, which was a common name among Spanish immigrants. Later, *dago* was also used for Italian and Portuguese immigrants.

STREET TYPES OF CHICAGO--CHARACTER STUDIES

IN THE EMPLOY OF THE GAS COMPANIES

COPYRIGHTED, 1891, BY *Krausz* 2930 COTTAGE GROVE AVE

The word *guinea* comes from the region in West Africa of the same name. It originally applied to a black person from Guinea, and was later used for Italians because they were noticeably foreign and frequently had dark hair, eyes, and complexions. *Wop* comes from a word in Sicilian and Neapolitan dialect, *guappo*, from the Spanish *guapo*, meaning handsome or dandy, but focusing on the disparaging meaning of dandy, that is, overdressed and foppish.

Other sources have other possible interpretations. The term *dago* may have originated because Italian immigrants were hired as day

laborers (as the "day goes"), or because hard-working, unhappy immigrants adopted the stoic philosophy of "Day come, *day go*." *Guinea* may have referred to the amount of money the Italian said he was working for: "A guinea a day."

At least one source translates *guappo* as "a boastful good-for-nothing," and says that Italian laborers in the nineteenth century were often represented by *padrones* (bosses) who acted as employment agents for a fee. The largest fees went to the workers the *padrone* identified as the biggest and strongest—as "guappo." One final

interpretation of *wop* says that it stood for without papers, since Italian immigrants would sometimes arrive with inadequate immigration papers.

(Above) **The original caption on this old photograph of Italian immigrant laborers working on the construction of the New Troy, Rens Pittsfield Electric Railway through the Lebanon Valley, New York, reads, "We no work now—stop and have picture took!" The stilted language emphasizes the stereotypical image of the "*dago*." Photo © Michael Maslan Historic Photographs/CORBIS.**

In October 1915, former president Theodore Roosevelt said—while speaking to the Knights of Columbus!—"There is no room in this country for hyphenated Americans. There is no such thing as a hyphenated American who is a good American." Also in 1915, President Wilson said that the "hyphenates have poured the poison of disloyalty into the very arteries of our national life.... Such creatures of passion, disloyalty, and anarchy must be crushed out." Yet Wilson vetoed more than one literacy bill that would have restricted immigration.

A backlash of World War I became evident when a "Nordic cult" revived the Ku Klux Klan in 1915. The new Klan opposed all foreigners, Negroes, Jews, and Catholics. Madison Grant, in his widely read book *The Passing of the Great Race*, wrote that Italians were inferior because when the ancient Romans died out they left only their slaves—who became those southern Italians seeking entrance to the United States.

Congress enacted the Literacy Bill of 1917 over Wilson's veto. The new bill affected southern Italians more than any other group of immigrants, and after thousands were barred, many Italian peasants studied to become literate before they attempted to emigrate to the United States. In December 1917 Congress proposed an amendment to the Constitution that would prohibit the manufacture, sale, or transportation of alcoholic beverages. It became the Eighteenth Amendment in January 1919. As usual, the plan was directed at the wine-loving Italians, and "to preserve the American way of life." Ironically, what Prohibition did was to strengthen organized crime in the United States, and its often Italian-American leaders, such as Al Capone. Another irony was that Italian Americans rarely drank outside the home, and so were not affected by Prohibition.

The Emergency Quota Act of 1921 was vetoed by President Wilson as he was leaving office, but then it was signed by incoming President Warren G. Harding. The quota law was meant to discriminate against southern and eastern Europeans. And it did. Italian immigrants were restricted to an annual limit of just over 42,000. On May 26, 1924, President Calvin Coolidge signed the Johnson Act into law, which lowered the immigration quotas

An Italian bootblack buying a Liberty Bond in New York City to support American troops in World War I, c. 1917. Italian Americans freely supported the United States during both world wars.

even further. On June 30 the quota for Italians was lowered from just over 42,000 to just over 3,800. The quota system was finally abolished in 1965.

In truth, many Italian immigrants did nothing to dispel the popular belief that they were a murderous and shifty bunch. Any prejudiced person looking for someone or something to attack could find a prime target in the Italian stereotype. After all, the nationalists reasoned, the homicide rate in southern Italy was the highest in Europe, and new stories of deadly vengeance in Italian ghettos in United States cities were rampant—hence, the connection was made to the lore of the Mafia and the Black Hand. Also, most immigrants from southern Italy had not seen much prosperity, giving credence to being labeled as aimless failures. Southern Italy was geographically closer to Africa than was England or Norway—hence, the accusation of being related to the black race. And on and on. Derogatory names were called—*dago, wop, guinea,* and worse—innocent men were sent to prison, and European Americans who had arrived in the United States before the Italians felt free to treat Italian workers like slaves.

Two devastating incidents illustrate the fever pitch of discrimination. One happened in the south, early in the tide of Italian immigration—1890—and the other happened in the north, as the tide was receding, in 1920. Both were indelible black marks on the history of America's treatment of its immigrants.

THE NEW ORLEANS MASSACRE

New Orleans had never been tolerant of Italian immigrants, especially Sicilians, who had established a large settlement in that city. The grumbling turned into violence in October 1890, when the superintendent of police —David C. Hennessey—was murdered during his investigation of rival Italian gangs. Before he died, Hennessey allegedly said, "The *dagos* did it." (Actually, Hennessey survived for several hours after the shooting, and when he was asked if he knew who shot him he nodded "no." It was only the word of Hennessey's friend, William O'Connor, that laid the blame on the Italians.)

The mayor of New Orleans ordered his police force to arrest every Italian they could find, and more than a hundred Italians were thrown into jail. Quickly, nine of the accused men were put on trial, despite evidence that some prominent citizens of New Orleans had been involved in the shooting. There were no Italians on the jury, and yet the case for the defense was so strong that the accused were still acquitted. But the discrimination did not stop after the "not guilty" verdict. Instead of being released after the trial, the nine Italians were returned to their prison cells, and the mayor called for a mass meeting "to take steps to remedy the failure of justice in the Hennessey case." He urged the citizens of New Orleans to "come prepared for action," and about ten thousand did just that.

(Opposite) **Nicola Sacco with his son and wife before his arrest, c. 1919. When there was a possibility of executing either Sacco or Vanzetti, Vanzetti volunteered to die in order to save Sacco's family.**

The mob tore down the prison gates and spread out to find the prisoners, whom the warden had released from their cells to fend for themselves. Six of the men were found hiding in the exercise courtyard, and were torn apart at close range by over a hundred rifle and gun shots. The crowd cheered. Three more Italians were located, and their heads were blown off. Two other men were hung and then used for target practice. Two of the eleven victims had not even been involved with the Hennessey case. Most of the mob that killed the Italians were leading members of New Orleans' press and political and business establishments, not the typical rabble of a mindless mob.

The next day, Senator Henry Cabot Lodge said that "the mob acted on the belief that these men were guilty of the crime with which they were charged; that the crime was the work of a secret society known as the Mafia; and that the failure of the jury to convict was due either to terror of this secret organization or to bribery [of the jury] by its agents." The same day *The New York Times* ran this approving headline: "Chief Hennessey Avenged. 11 of His Italian Assassins Lynched by Mob."

Lynching of Italians in the south occurred sporadically for the next twenty years, and southern laws severely restricted the arrival of more Italian immigrants. ("Citizens of Ireland, Scotland, Switzerland, and France, together with all other foreigners of Saxon origin" were welcome.) Needless to say, Italian immigrants began to avoid the American south.

SACCO AND VANZETTI

The Bolshevik Revolution of 1917, together with America's entry into World War I, unnerved many Americans who felt they had good reason to crack down on so-called radicals. Attorney General A. Mitchell Palmer began proceedings against thousands of suspected radicals and the activity he defined as "a distinctly criminal and dishonest movement in the desire to obtain possession of other people's property by violence and robbery." These "Red" radicals included Socialists, Communists, Anarchists, and anyone who opposed the war. The "Palmer Raids" had begun, and the call was out for a national standard of "100 percent Americanism."

A 1927 photograph of Vanzetti and Sacco handcuffed to a guard and each other while awaiting a court appearance during their prolonged appeal, a month before the executions.

It was in this seething "Red Scare" atmosphere that the Italian immigrants Nicola Sacco and Bartolomeo Vanzetti found themselves on May 5, 1920, when they were arrested at gunpoint and charged with the murders of Frederick A. Parmenter, a shoe factory paymaster, and Alessandro Berardelli, a guard, during a robbery of more than fifteen thousand dollars in South Braintree, Massachusetts, in April.

When Sacco and Vanzetti were arrested they were both armed, and both were admitted draft dodgers and anarchists, but this did not necessarily mean that they were terrorists or murderers. For them, and for many other countryless immigrants, anarchism (they did not call it "anarchy") was a core belief that gave their lives meaning. They believed in human dignity, freedom, and justice. Anarchism made the Italians feel superior to the materialists who scorned them as ignorant and shiftless. Although neither Sacco nor Vanzetti was a leader, both were active in working-class organizations. It is interesting that both Sacco and Vanzetti learned their anar-chism in the United States. Nicola Sacco had come to the United States in 1908, when he was seventeen, from a poor agricultural town, Torremag-giore. In his early days in Boston he worked as a waterboy and laborer, later learning the trade of an edge trimmer in a shoe factory. Married and with a son, he worked hard to support his family. Bartolomeo Vanzetti was born in Piedmont, where he was apprenticed to a baker and pastry maker. He arrived in America in 1908 at age twenty-four and earned his living first as a kitchen helper and laborer, and then as a fish peddler. Without family, his social life consisted of meeting with anarchist friends, including Sacco, with whom he often spent the day splitting wood and "speaking about many things."

Another friend of Sacco and Vanzetti was Andrea Salsedo, a Brooklyn printer who also published an underground newsletter that revealed that a government agent posing as an anarchist had precipitated middle-of-the-night arrests of anarchists without due process of law. Salsedo was arrested and held incommunicado in the offices of the Department of Justice. Sacco and Vanzetti went to New York and found out that Salsedo had been tor-tured, and was given an attorney who had turned out to be an agent of the Department of Justice.

Vanzetti returned to Boston and advised his fellow anarchists to prepare to be raided. Shortly afterward, Salsedo either jumped or was pushed to his death from the fourteenth-floor window of the Justice Department's offices. Two days later, on May 5, 1920, Sacco and Vanzetti were arrested while trying to recover anarchist literature they had already distributed. Both men were taken to the jail in Brockton, Massachusetts.

The case against Sacco and Vanzetti began on May 31, 1921, in Dedham, Massachusetts, and was tried before Webster Thayer, a notoriously preju-diced judge, by an aggressive prosecutor who played to all the prevailing fears and hatreds of the time, and before a jury chosen from a population that largely shared the judge's public viewpoint that the United States was being threatened by foreigners and "Reds." The trial pitted two immigrant workers against all those of power and authority who felt threatened by the labor violence of the preceding years, which was perceived by them as a world conspiracy headed by Russian revolutionaries. The fact that these two Italians were as intellectually and socially aware as the most educated American was another source of fear and resentment. Before sentencing, Sacco said, "I never know, never heard, even read in history anything so cruel as this court. I know the sentence will be between two class, the oppressed class and the rich class.... This is why I am here today on this bench, for having been the oppressed class. Well, you are the oppressor."

Vanzetti said, "Not only am I innocent of these two crimes [he had been convicted—apparently without justification—of an unrelated crime before the Dedham trial began], not only in all my life I have never stole, never killed, never spilled blood, but I have struggled all my life...to eliminate crime from the earth.... I am suffering because I am a radical and indeed I am a radical; I have suffered because I was an Italian, and indeed I am an Italian.... I am so convinced to be right that you could execute me two times, and if I could be reborn two other times, I would live again to do what I have done already. I have finished. Thank you."

Despite only circumstantial evidence and the testimony of witnesses who swore that Sacco and Vanzetti were not at the scene of the crime, the Italians were found guilty in July 1921 and sentenced to death. During almost seven years on death row, passionate protests demanding freedom and justice took place all over the world. Judge Thayer managed to effectively block a retrial, and the Lowell Committee—named after A. Lawrence Lowell, president of Harvard University and an early supporter of restricting the entry of immigrants—that was appointed by Governor Alvan T. Fuller to study the case upheld Fuller's earlier refusal of clemency.

Sacco and Vanzetti were electrocuted on August 23, 1927.

We will never know for sure if Sacco and Vanzetti were guilty, but we can be certain that legal representatives of the state of Massachusetts acted

more like persecutors than prosecutors, and that *prejudiced* in this emotion-filled case truly meant "pre-judged."

On August 23, 1977, exactly fifty years after the controversial execution, Massachusetts Governor Michael Dukakis issued a proclamation that Sacco and Vanzetti had been tried improperly. It went practically unnoticed.

ITALIAN AMERICANS AND WORLD WAR II

Italian Americans served in World War I and supported the Allied effort in any other way they could. When Benito Mussolini began his rise to power in Italy in the 1920s Italian Americans supported him because they hoped

The street-lined funeral procession of Sacco and Vanzetti, Boston, 1927. Public protests began at the beginning of the trial and continued after the executions. In a sense, they continue today. Photo © UPI/Corbis-Bettmann.

The Italian Immigrants on "The Hill," the well-known Italian-American section of St. Louis.

Mrs. Rosario Clemenza, who emigrated from Italy in 1919, seen here with her American-born son Anthony in 1939 in Brooklyn. Anthony is helping his mother learn English by reading from the local news-paper. This daily ritual was prescribed by the judge who ruled that Mrs. Clemenza must be more proficient in English before she could be presented with her final U.S. citizenship papers. Photo © UPI/Corbis-Bettmann.

his policies would help their relatives in Italy. Also, the immigrants believed that Italy's expansion into Abyssinia, Ethiopia, and Somaliland would add to the pride of Italians everywhere. But these feelings of support changed when World War II began and Mussolini aligned himself alongside Hitler, and once again Italian Americans placed their loyalty firmly with their adopted country, not Italy. The choice was surprisingly easy for the Italians in America, who looked at their children and realized that the future lay with the young, not with the old, and with a democracy that fulfilled its promises, not with elitism that ignored them and a fascism that lied.

When Italy became a foe of the United States during World War II the government ordered all Italian immigrants to register as enemy aliens. After a short period during which Italian Americans were considered suspicious and banned from restricted areas, the bans were dropped.

Italian Americans were unquestionably loyal to the United States and believed that Mussolini had acted foolishly in entering the war as an Axis power. On Columbus Day, 1942, United States Attorney General Francis

U.S. Army Air Corps Captain Don S. Gentile, of Italian descent, receiving the Distinguished Service Cross from General Dwight D. Eisenhower, supreme Allied commander on the western front *(right)*. Gentile is credited with destroying thirty German planes, the highest record made by an American fighter pilot in Europe. *(Below)* Gentile's faithful mascot Bobo proudly shares the cockpit.

Biddle stated that his department had found Italian Americans to be totally loyal to their new country. After an intense ten-month investigation only about two hundred Italians were interned, or about one-twentieth of one percent of the entire Italian population in the United States. The label of "enemy alien" was lifted, and Italian Americans went on to be strong supporters of the United States war effort, whether they were fighting in the military or remaining at home as civilians.

Thanksgiving dinner at Grandma's house was an annual tradition for this still-growing Italian-American family (note the two "war babies"), but 1945 was a special year. All three sons (in uniform) who had served in combat during the war had returned home safely. The proud patriarch is barely seen at the far left, smoking a celebratory cigar. Grandma is in the center of the photo, above her sailor son.

A CLOSER LOOK:
THE BLACK HAND
AND THE MAFIA

Apparently, the notion that there was such an organization as the "Black Hand" originated in Andalusia, Spain, in the early 1880s. Landowners there suspected that the secret organization had been formed to destroy them. The matter was investigated, and little or no evidence of the Black Hand was found, but nevertheless the known anarchists in the region were condemned.

The path from Spaniards to Italians—both considered "*dagos*"—was a short one, and soon the myth of the Black Hand had spread to Italy, where once again there was no evidence to prove the organization existed. Still, the press fanned the flames, and the myth grew.

The so-called Mafia has had a similar background. Because of foreign rule, the danger of invasion, and unfair laws, a few Sicilians formed bands of rebels who went about righting political wrongs. Included in the system was the code of silence, or *omerta*, which forbade anyone from giving information to the police.

Originally, the rebel groups asked for money from those they protected, and eventually a criminal element demanded money whether or not it provided protection. Whatever else is known about the Sicilian Mafia, it seems clear that it was not highly organized and was limited to northern Sicily.

Italian immigrants as a group had a lower crime rate than other immigrants, and the crimes they committed were usually petty ones such as gambling or fighting. For all the talk about the criminal tendencies of Italian immigrants it was only in New York City (primarily because of Mulberry Bend) that the Italians' arrest rate was a slight 0.8 percent higher than the average.

Many sociologists believe that the Mafia in the United States is a creation of Americans, exaggerated in the press, novels, movies, and television, and although there is organized crime in the United States it is not as hierarchical as we are led to believe. Fortunately, discrimination against Italian Americans and the notion of an organized, Italian-driven Mafia is decreasing. But alas, the Corleone clan does make for a good story.

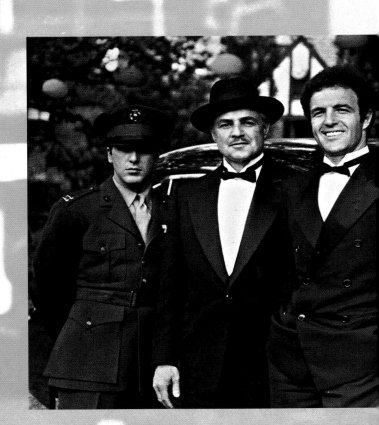

(Background) Actor Robert DeNiro on the set of *The Godfather, Part II*, released in 1974, in which he played the part of the young Vito Corleone, before he matured into the "godfather," the role originated by Marlon Brando in *The Godfather* in 1972.

(Above left) Publicity still of Al Pacino, Marlon Brando, James Caan, and John Cazale on the movie set of *The Godfather*, 1972.

(Below left) The famous wedding scene from *The Godfather*, 1972.

ITALIAN AMERICANS MAKE THEIR MARK

I t has been over five hundred years since Columbus sailed to the New World, and we can look back at the adventurers, explorers, musicians, painters, sculptors, artisans, and the great mass of workers who came to America for a better life. Although they may have felt a deep yearning for their home roots in Italy, they found a new place in America as safe as any home could be. And they all contributed to help form the character of America.

In 1910 Italian Americans were the lowest paid workers in the United States, averaging $10.50 a week when the average American wage was $14.37—27 percent higher. For many Italian immigrants, however, $10.50 a week was an improvement over the impoverished conditions they had come from. It took a while, but they kept improving their situation until most of them had risen to heights few had dreamed possible, achieving success in all walks of life. This chapter highlights some of the Italian Americans who have become American heroes in their chosen fields.

BUSINESS

Although many Italian immigrants started as pushcart peddlers, many of them soon began their own small businesses, which were often related to food. An extremely successful case was that of Amadeo Obici, who came to the United States in 1889 when he was twelve, and opened a fruit stand at

(Opposite) **Amadeo Peter Giannini, founder of the Bank of Italy (which became the Bank of America), boosts young actor Jackie Coogan to the bank teller's window to deposit his paycheck.**

(Previous spread) **Fruits and vegetables being sold on outdoor pushcarts, c. 1950. The Italian-American diet continued to include many varieties of fresh fruits and vegetables.**

A CLOSER LOOK:
A.P. GIANNINI: BANKER TO THE WORKING CLASS

Opportunities in California for Italian immigrants were often greater than those in the eastern cities, and these opportunities were not limited to fishing, farming, and winemaking.

Amadeo Peter (A.P.) Giannini (*photo below*) had a head start, having been born in 1870 in San Jose, California, of immigrant parents from Genoa. Apart from other children of Italian immigrants he developed an interest in how American banks could help Italian Americans who could not, or would not, obtain loans from local banks. In 1904, at the age of thirty-four, he founded the Bank of Italy in the Italian section of North Beach in San

Francisco (*picture above*), hiring Italian-speaking tellers and initiating such services as free help with naturalization papers, branch banking, and open patronage to all Italians, not just *paesani*, as was the custom with other Italian banks.

Two years after founding the Bank of Italy, the great earthquake struck San Francisco in the early morning hours, and Giannini literally rolled out of bed, dressed quckly, and did what for him was to become typical behavior. He hitched a team of horses to a produce wagon and drove downtown to his bank, which was in rubbles. Before looters were even aware that an earthquake had struck, Giannini pored over the ruins of his bank and loaded about $2 million in gold, coins, and securities into the wagon. He covered the treasure with the vegetables in the wagon, and calmly drove home.

But A. P. Giannini's heroics did not stop there. With his concern for the working-class people of San Francisco, he set up a "bank" on the docks—a wooden plank stretched over two barrels—and began extending credit to working people who needed money to recover from the devastating earthquake *(opposite page)*. Other banks were in favor of staying closed during this emergency period, but soon the entire city rallied around Giannini's example and began to rebuild. In that same spirit of selflessness, Giannini pioneered the concept of home mortgages and other installment-

type loans that enabled immigrants to buy their own homes, automobiles, and small businesses. Of course, he was aware of the needs of big business too, helping to start the California wine industry, and, establishing a special motion-picture loan division that helped Mary Pickford, Charlie Chaplin, Douglas Fairbanks, and D. W. Griffith create United Artists, the first film studio owned by actors and a director.

In 1928 Giannini had bought the Bank of America, and by 1945 it became the largest bank in the United States. And when Walt Disney needed help to complete his dream–to make the first full-length animated film– Bank of America stepped in. Disney was able to finish *Snow White and the Seven Dwarfs*. When Giannini died in 1949, the assets of the Bank of America were valued at $5

billion, but his own estate was worth less than half a million dollars, as a result of his having preferred to stay close to the people by receiving virtually no pay and typically donating a $1.5 million bonus to the University of California. He said, "I have worked without thinking of myself. This is the largest factor in whatever success I have attained."

In 1999, the Bank of America had assets of $572 billion, making it the second largest bank in the United States behind Citicorp, with $751 billion.

A CLOSER LOOK:
ROBERT MONDAVI: MASTER VINTNER, FAMILY WINEMAKER

The California wines of the Robert Mondavi Winery, first produced in 1966, have since taken their place among the finest premium American wines. Mondavi, born in 1913, is no new-comer to fine wines. His parents emigrated from Italy to the United States in 1910 and soon became involved in arranging for California wine grapes to be shipped to Italian immigrants who made their own wine.

In 1923, when Robert was ten years old, the family moved to California and began a full-scale business of shipping California wine grapes to the eastern United States. Robert immediately became immersed in the family business, and after graduating

from Stanford University in 1936 he joined his father and two employees in the production of California wine. In 1943, Robert convinced his father to purchase the Charles Krug Winery, and the many innovations that were to distinguish the future Robert Mondavi Winery had begun.

Mondavi has succeeded in producing world-class wines, and he has done it with the help of his entire family. Robert is chairman

of the board. His eldest son, Michael, is president and CEO; his son Timothy is managing director and winegrower; his daughter, Marcia, is on the board of directors; and his wife, Margrit Biever, is vice president of cultural affairs, and developed the company's Summer Music Festival, the Festival of Winter Classical Concerts, and a fine-arts gallery. She also originated the Great Chefs programs at the Mondavi winery. The Mondavi family is committed to carry on this tradition of excellence for generations to come.

Robert Mondavi's courage and originality led the way for other enterprising American vintners—including filmmaker Francis Ford Coppola—and has proved once and for all that some of the finest wines in the world can be produced in the United States.

Robert Mondavi, seen opposite, with sons Michael, president and CEO of Robert Mondavi Winery, and Timothy, managing director and winegrower. The lush entrance to the vineyard is shown above.

Mountains of spaghetti;
Pie in the sky. . . .
Pasta and pizza are probably two of the most popular "ethnic" foods. What would we do without the Italian influence on our palates?

(*Above*) The Atlantic Macaroni Company, makers of Caruso brand products, 1943. Raking the spaghetti actually helps to keep it from clogging the operation.

(*Left*) Patsy's Pizzeria, the first pizzeria in New York, opened in East Harlem in 1933 after Patsy Lancieri, an early Italian immigrant, perfected his recipe for "New York Style pizza" in the salumerias of Little Italy. His authentic old-world pizza established Patsy as New York's foremost pizza baker, inspiring scores of imitators. The famous Patsy's remained a favorite spot for generations of long-time pizza lovers.

In the 1990's the new owners of Patsy's opened several pizzerias throughout the city, in the tradition of the original in East Harlem. They still proudly serve Patsy Lancieri's old world recipe.

seventeen, where he specialized in peanuts when he discovered that Americans were willing to pay a nickel for roasted and packaged peanuts. He started his peanut business with a roaster and a sign over his stand: OBICI, THE PEANUT SPECIALIST. In each package of peanuts he put a coupon bearing a letter of the alphabet; anyone who collected coupons that spelled the name OBICI was given a watch.

When Obici expanded to candy bars and business flourished, his landlords raised his rents, so Obici went into the real estate business to buy his own buildings, even buying farmlands in Virginia, where he grew his own peanuts, and producting tin for his canned peanuts. Obici founded the Planters Peanut Corporation, and became a model for entrepreneurial Italian Americans.

Andrea Sbarboro was born near Genoa and came to the United States as a child with his parents, settling in San Francisco. After working as everything from a store clerk to a successful banker, Sbarboro started a community to establish vineyards at Asti, California, and a few years later, in 1890, he formed the Italian Swiss Colony wine company, so named because some of the workers came from the Italian-speaking section of Switzerland.

Joseph and Rosario diGiorgio developed large fruit orchards in the San Joaquin Valley in California, and ultimately became the world's largest shippers of fresh fruit; they canned their fruit under the S&W label. Julio and Ernest Gallo currently produce almost half of all California wines. California's Robert Mondavi Vineyards has become well known as one of the country's premier vintners. Marco J. Fontana, a Ligurian who arrived in the United States in 1859, founded the California Fruit Packing Corporation, which went on to become the largest fruit and vegetable canning company in the world. With Antonio Cerruti, Fontana started the canning company that became Del Monte.

Amadeo Peter Giannini founded the Bank of Italy, which later became the Bank of America. Without the Bank of Italy, many vineyards—and Holly-

Lee Iacocca as the grand marshall of the 1982 Columbus Day parade. Iacocca became a model for many Italian-American businessmen. Photo © Jacques M. Chenet/ CORBIS.

wood movies—would not have been possible. Giannini provided critical funding to finish *Gone With the Wind*.

A huge success story in another field, Lee (Lido Anthony) Iacocca is the son of Italian immigrants from San Marco in the province of Campania. He grew up in Allentown, Pennsylvania, and eventually made an astounding success in the automobile business, serving first as the president of the Ford Motor Company and then as the CEO of the Chrysler Corporation, where he was instrumental in saving Chrysler from bankruptcy and helping it regain its first-class stature as a manufacturer of fine automobiles. President Reagan appointed Iacocca chairman of the Statue of Liberty-Ellis Island Centennial Commission.

Other Italian Americans extremely successful in the business world include Frank J. Biondi, Jr., chairman and CEO of Universal Studios; Livia D. DeSimone, chairman and CEO of 3M Corporation; Richard A. Grasso, chairman and CEO of the New York Stock Exchange; Phil Guarascio, general manager and vice president of General Motors; Frank Mancuso, chairman and CEO of MGM; Tommy Mottola, president and CEO of Sony Music Entertainment; Carleton Fiorina, president and CEO of Hewlett-Packard; and Lucio A. Noto, chairman and CEO of Mobil Corporation. A most impressive list.

Fiorello LaGuardia checks the voting returns that recorded his successful nomination as the continuing Republican candidate for mayor of New York City, 1941.

POLITICS

The ever-ready Mayor LaGuardia leading a municipal band during the "I Am An American Day" celebration in New York.

Although few early Italian Americans ran for public office, they caught up with a vengeance with the "Little Flower." Fiorello H. LaGuardia had the perfect background and temperament for New York City. He was born in a Greenwich Village tenement in 1882 to an agnostic Italian father and an Austrian Jewish mother. He spoke English, Italian, Yiddish, Hungarian, German, Serbian, Croatian, and Spanish. He was raised in Arizona and lived as a young man in Europe, but he returned to New York at twenty-three, where he eventually became an interpreter at Ellis Island while he earned his law degree in the evenings at NYU. His specialty was immigration law. His first wife was a Catholic, but after she died he married a Lutheran. He was a Mason and an Episcopalian.

LaGuardia received his law degree and was admitted to the bar in 1910 at the age of twenty-eight, quickly establishing himself as a champion of the poor and helpless. He spent his career trying to aid the underprivileged of urban America. He lost his first bid for the U.S. House of Representatives, but was appointed as deputy attorney general of New York State. In 1916 he won a seat in Congress—the first Republican to serve his district since the Civil War—and became an outspoken advocate of reform. When the United States entered World War I he took a leave of absence and enlisted in the army as a first lieutenant. Before the war ended he was a major.

Upon returning to civilian life he won his old seat in Congress in a landslide, but soon left at the urging of New York City Republican leaders to run for the office of president of the Board of Aldermen, with the understanding that he would run for mayor in the next election. He won the election as president of the Board of Aldermen of New York City—second only to the office of mayor—and became the "man of the moment" in gaining the highest elected position of any Italian American in a major city. But he clashed with party leaders and was denied the mayoral nomination they had promised. Instead, he won back his congressional seat and served there from 1923 to 1933, when he was finally elected mayor of New York City, winning against the tide of FDR's success. LaGuardia was sworn in as mayor of New York City on January 1, 1934, but he was not the first Italian American to become mayor of a major American city; that honor went to Angelo Rossi of San Francisco in 1931.

LaGuardia's most important piece of legislation while a congressman was the Norris-LaGuardia Anti-Injunction Act, which was signed into law by President Hoover in 1932. The act established the right of American labor to bargain collectively, and prohibited courts from issuing strike injunctions unless management could demonstrate that it had already bargained honestly, and protected workers in many other ways. Many considered the Norris-LaGuardia Act to be labor's Magna Carta.

LaGuardia served New York City as mayor with great flair and distinction for twelve years. But he surely solidified his place in history when during a

Republican Congress-
man Peter Rodino of
New Jersey (*left:*)
served as chairman of
the House Judiciary
Committee during the
Watergate hearings,
and Federal Judge
John J. Sirica (*right:*
photo © UPI/Corbis-
Bettmann) presided
over the Watergate
case. Both men were
instrumental in the
resolution of President
Nixon's political prob-
lems.

New York City newspaper strike he went on the radio to read the Sunday comics to the deprived youngsters of New York. His readings were chillingly dramatic, and he used a different falsetto voice for every cartoon character. (Every political speech he ever made was given in a falsetto voice that boomed out of his tiny, squat body.) No listener, young or old, will ever forget those readings, which were then shown in newsreels all over the country, and which obviously brought as much joy to LaGuardia as his happy listeners.

The Broadway musical *Fiorello* paid him a lighthearted tribute, and of course, LaGuardia Airport is named after him.

The Little Flower died in 1947, one of New York's—and the country's—most unforgettable characters.

The first Italian-American presidential cabinet member was Anthony J. Celebrezze, who in 1962 was appointed by President Kennedy to be his secretary of Health, Education, and Welfare. Previously Celebrezze had served five terms as mayor of Cleveland.

In 1946 John Pastore of Rhode Island became the first Italian American to become governor; he already had had the honor of being the first Italian-American senator.

Other outstanding Italian-American politicians include Joseph Alioto, mayor of San Francisco; Alfonse M. D'Amato, senator from New York; Pete V. Domenici, senator from New Mexico; Senator Mike Enzi from Wyoming; Governor James Florio of New Jersey; Rudolph Giuliani, mayor

(Above) **Ella Grasso, the former governor of Connecticut. Photo © Bettmann/CORBIS.**

(Opposite, bottom) **Geraldine Ferraro, Democratic congresswoman from the state of New York, was the first woman to be nominated for the vice-presidency of the United States, chosen by running mate Walter Mondale. Photo © Jacques M. Chenet/ CORBIS.**

of New York; Senator Patrick Leahy from Vermont; Romano Mazzoli, congressman from Kentucky; Congresswoman Susan Molinari from New York City, who was the youngest member of Congress when she was elected in 1990; Leon Panetta and John Podesta, both chiefs of staff to President Clinton; Senator Robert Torricelli of New Jersey; and John Volpe, governor of Massachusetts.

Mario Matthew Cuomo was born in the borough of Queens in New York City in 1932, the son of Andrea and Immaculata Cuomo, who had emigrated to the United States from Salerno in the 1920s. Once in the United

New York Governor Mario Cuomo, a master speechmaker and debater, and one of the country's most successful governors.

States, the Cuomos opened an Italian-American grocery store in South Jamaica, Queens.

Cuomo graduated from St. John's University summa cum laude, in 1953, where he had been awarded a scholarship to play varsity baseball. He had received a minor-league baseball contract with the Pittsburgh Pirates after his high-school graduation, but he decided to attend college and pursue a career in law instead. He was admitted to the New York bar in 1956, after being tied for top class honors at St. John's Law School, and soon after entered the world of politics.

Cuomo attracted public attention in 1972 as a legal mediator, when he settled a bitter housing dispute in New York City between blacks and Jews. From 1975 to 1979 he was New York's secretary of state, lieutenant governor from 1979 to 1982, and governor from 1983 to 1994, the longest tenure of any Democratic governor in the modern history of New York State. As governor of New York, Cuomo guided the state through two recessions, balanced twelve consecutive budgets, created more than half a million jobs, launched the largest economic development in New York history, and created the country's most extensive drug-treatment network.

After an unsuccessful run at the presidential nomination he became an elegant spokesman for the Democratic party, and he has continued in that capacity into the twenty-first century. Since leaving elective office, Cuomo has become a partner in the New York law firm of Wilkie, Farr, and Gallagher, where he specializes in national and international corporate law.

Antonin Scalia is the only Italian-American justice of the United States Supreme Court, a major honor. Photo © Reuters/Corbis-Bettmann.

The author of several books and articles, Cuomo, in 1997, became with William Bennett, the co-chairman of the Partnership for a Drug-Free America.

Mario Cuomo's son, Andrew M. Cuomo, served in the Clinton cabinet as secretary of Housing and Urban Development, and is married to Kerry Kennedy, the daughter of Robert F. Kennedy.

Like Joe DiMaggio before him, Mario Cuomo represents dignity to Italian Americans. He once said, "There's a difference between being tough and being loud." He has always been the former and never the latter. Always a spiritual intellectual, he believes that "politics is the highest vocation after the religious vocation, because the business of politics and government is to distribute the goods of the world in such a way as to improve the condition of people's lives."

SPORTS

From the beginning the children of Italian immigrants eagerly took part in the games and sports of America, especially baseball. The Catholic Church played an important role in the development of ethnic ballplayers among the poor. Babe Ruth owed his start to Brother Matthias Boutier of St. Mary's Industrial School in Baltimore, and in the Italian section of St. Louis called "Dago Hill," Father Causino, a third-generation Bohemian, Italianized his name from Kaceno and learned to speak Italian to be able to work with the youth of his parish. Father Causino was aware of gang violence on "The Hill," and devoted himself to direct that energy into sports.

The first Italian-sounding name to appear in the baseball records was Tony DeFate, who played with the Detroit Tigers in 1917, compiling the unenviable batting average of .127. In 1911 Ping Bodie (whose real name was either Giuseppe or Francesco Pezzolo) played for the Chicago White Sox, and batted a respectable .287. Later, Bodie played with the Philadelphia A's and the New York Yankees, where his roommate was Babe Ruth. Bodie said, almost as a foretaste of Yogi Berra's unwittingly witty sayings years later, "I

don't room with the Babe; I room with his bags." It was rumored that it was Bodie who first called Ruth the "Bambino," creating the welcome but improbable notion among Italian immigrants that the Babe was Italian.

Italian-American baseball players came to prominence in the mid-1920s, when outstanding players like Tony Lazzeri (a future Hall-of-Famer) played with the Yankees, and Ernie Orsatti batted .306 with the St. Louis Browns. Many of the early Italian players came to the Browns, whose policy was to sign up as many players as cheaply as possible, sell those who did well to other teams, and discard the rest. Among the players who came up via this route was Gus Mancuso, who later had a long career with the New York Giants, and Joe Cicero of Boston. Many of the discarded players returned to the brickyards of St. Louis or the fields of California.

Francesco (Frankie) Crosetti was born in San Francisco in 1910, and began his major-league career with the Yankees in 1932. After his playing days were over he became a Yankee coach for many years, helping to develop

Group portrait of the Stags Jrs. Athletic Club baseball team, which played in the YMCA league in St. Louis; c. 1938. The photo is noteworthy because two of the young teammates, residents of the Italian-American section known as "The Hill," are Yogi Berra (third from left, middle row) and Joe Garagiola (left, front row). Both boys went on to play in the major leagues, and remained close friends all their lives.

New York Yankee shortstop Phil Rizzuto takes time out from a brand-new career in the major leagues (which would lead to the Hall of Fame) to get married to his wife Cora and to serve (less voluntarily) in the U.S. Navy during World War II.

other Italian-American Yankee players. Baseball's Hall of Fame includes Lawrence "Yogi" Berra, Roy Campanella (half-Italian), Joe DiMaggio, Tony Lazzeri, Ernie Lombardi, and Phil Rizzuto. To illustrate what a magnet New York City is for Italian Americans, *all* of those Hall-of-Famers played in New York City, and Berra, Rizzuto, and DiMaggio all played with the New York Yankees *at the same time.*

The 1930s brought stand-out players such as New York Giants catcher/slugger Ernie Lombardi. Lombardi was so slow that when he laid down a successful bunt one day, the tabloid newspaper headline screamed, "LOMBARDI BEATS OUT BUNT." A triple was another rarity for the lumbering Hall-of-Famer.

Other outstanding Italian-American baseball players include Johnny Antonelli, Rocky Colavito, Tony Conigliaro, Vic Lombardi, Mike Mussina, Mike Piazza, Dave Righetti, Frank Torre, and Robin Ventura. Among Italian-American umpires are "Babe" Pinelli (Renaldo Angelo Paolinelli) and Steve Palermo.

Toward the end of the twentieth century Italian-American athletes were moving up into managerial and administrative positions when their playing

Mike Mussina is a perennial All-Star pitcher for the Baltimore Orioles. As of the end of the 1999 season he owned the lowest earned-run average of all active pitchers. Photo © Jerry Wachter.

A CLOSER LOOK:
JOLTIN' JOE DIMAGGIO: WE HAD YOU ON OUR SIDE

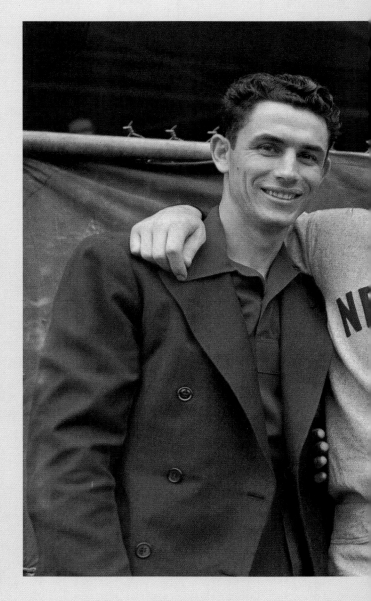

None of us knew Joe DiMaggio. Most of us never even saw him play baseball. And yet, none of us will ever forget him. Why? Maybe because he represented a trait dear to Italian Americans, a trait that many immigrants wanted for their children: Joe DiMaggio was *civile*. He was dignified, and he helped change the way Americans thought about Italians.

Joseph Paul DiMaggio was born on November 25, 1914, in Martinez, California, a small fishing village just north of San Francisco. That same year, the family moved to North Beach, the Italian section near the wharves of San Francisco. His father was a crab fisherman who had emigrated to the United States in 1898 from a small island off Sicily, and Joe's older brothers also became fishermen. But not Joe.

He began his professional baseball career with the San Francisco Seals, one of the best minor league teams, in 1932 when he was seventeen years old. The next year he batted .340 and hit safely in sixty-one consecutive games, and in the following two years he batted .341 and .398. He was still just twenty-one years old when the New York Yankees bought his contract from the Seals; in his first year in the big leagues, 1936, playing with future Hall-of-Famers Lou Gehrig, Tony Lazzeri, Lefty Gomez, Red Ruffing, and Bill Dickey, DiMaggio held his own nicely, batting an amazing .323. (He was the first rookie to ever start in an All-Star game.) The Yankees went on to win the World Series in 1936, with DiMaggio batting .346. But greatness wasn't enough for the national press; *Life* magazine showed that the nation hadn't fully accepted Italian Americans when it reported in a supposedly favorable article in 1939, "Although he learned Italian first, Joe, now 24, speaks English without an accent, and is otherwise well adapted to most U.S. mores. Instead of olive oil or smelly bear grease he keeps his hair slick with water. He never reeks of garlic and prefers chicken chow mein to spaghetti." If Joe noticed, he never let on. He remained, as always, *civile*.

DiMaggio's baseball statistics are among the best, with a lifetime batting average of .325. In 1941 he put together a fifty-six-game consecutive hitting streak that many experts consider the one baseball record that will stand forever—and bandleader Les Brown recorded the hit song, "Joltin' Joe DiMaggio... we want you on our side." DiMaggio was also the smoothest outfielder of his day, but manager Joe McCarthy pointed out one of Joe's overlooked skills when he said, "He was the best base runner I ever saw.... He wasn't the fastest man alive. He just knew how to run bases better than anybody." And longtime teammate Tommy Henrich paid him perhaps the greatest compliment, saying with awe, "I never saw him make a mistake."

In DiMaggio's thirteen years with the New York Yankees, the team appeared in ten World Series; they won nine times.

A proud man in a private way, DiMaggio was publicly proud of being voted Baseball's Greatest Living Player in 1969. Now he would have to relinquish that title, probably to Ted Williams or Willie Mays. Joe DiMaggio died on March 8, 1999, and we all wished him Godspeed. And, Joe, thanks for the memories.

(*Below*) **A young Joe DiMaggio pleases his mother by eating a huge plate of pasta at the family home in North Beach, California, c. 1936. Photo © UPI/Corbis–Bettmann.**

(*Left*) **Joe with brothers Vincent (left) and Dominic, both of whom played in the major leagues at the same time as Joe. Vince spent his career in the National League, but Dom played for the rival Boston Red Sox, 1940. Photo © Bettmann/CORBIS.**

DiMaggio was injured early and often in his career, but he was usually able to play through the pain. But finally, even Ernest Hemingway could see that Joe wasn't healthy, and wrote about the fragility of greatness in *The Old Man and the Sea*, when the tired old fisherman has been out in his little boat day after day without success: "This is the second day now that I do not know the result of the juegos [baseball games]. But I must have confidence and I must be worthy of the Great DiMaggio who does all things perfectly even with the pain of the bone spur in his heel." DiMaggio retired in 1951 and in 1955 was elected into the Hall of Fame.

DiMaggio had married Marilyn Monroe in 1954, but in his old–fashioned Italian way he was never reconciled to the idea of his wife being worshipped as a sex goddess, and they were divorced that same year.

The powerful follow-through of Joe DiMaggio signals another hard line drive to left field.

Gene Sarazen (Eugene Saraceni) is only one of four golfers to win all four major professional golf tournaments; U. S. Open in 1922 and 1932; PGA Championship in 1922, 1923, and 1933; British Open in 1932; and the Masters in 1935.

days were over. Tommy Lasorda started as a mediocre pitcher in the Dodger organization and eventually became one of the Los Angeles Dodgers' most successful (not to mention charismatic) managers. Other ballplayers who rose to the position of manager were Joe Torre, Billy Martin (Alfred Manuel Pesano), Jim Fregosi, Bobby Valentine, and Tony LaRussa.

An example of how professional sports was trying to improve its image was the hiring of former president of Yale University A. (Angelo) Bartlett (an obvious echo of Bartolomeo) Giamatti in 1986 as the president of the National League of Major League Baseball. An ardent baseball fan since his boyhood in South Hadley, Massachusetts, Giamatti formed his own Italian-American All-Star baseball team: catcher, Yogi Berra; first base, Dolph Camilli; second base, Tony Lazzeri; shortstop, Phil Rizzuto; third base,

Frank Crosetti; outfielders, Joe DiMaggio, Dom DiMaggio, Sam Mele, Al "Zeke" Zarilla, and Carl Furillo; and pitchers Vic Raschi and Sal Maglie. Giamatti's Italian-American dream team spanned the three decades when the children of immigrants began to make a major mark in sports.

By the time many Italian-Americas had become successful in baseball, others began appearing on the college and professional football fields of America. At the University of Chicago were Felix Caruso and Adolphe Toigio; of Toigio coach Amos Alonzo Stagg said, "He was one of the three immortals." At Notre Dame, the "Fighting Irish" had two Italian-American stars coached by Knute Rockne, Frank Cardeo and Joe Savoldi, and at Columbia University during the 1930s and 1940s Luigi Piccolo coached under the soon-to-be-famous name of Lou Little.

Jockey Eddie Arcaro, seen here winning on horse number 3, was the first jockey to win racing's triple crown twice, in 1941 and 1948.

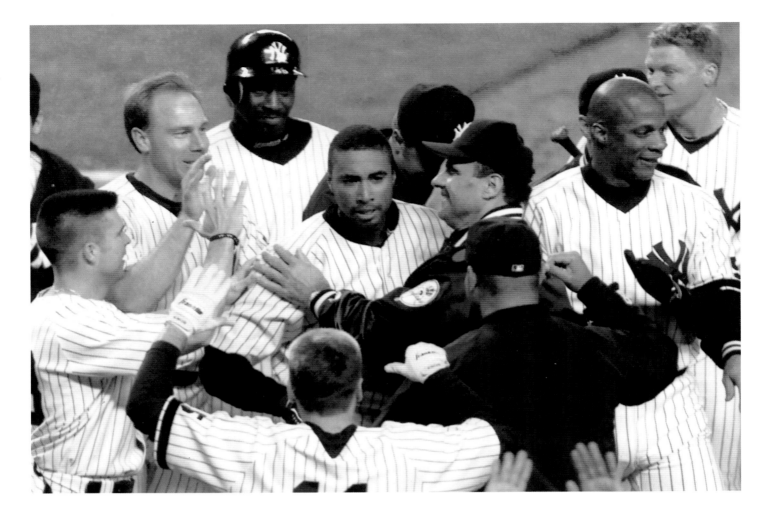

Man-of-the-hour Joe Torre, pride of Italian Americans everywhere, is surrounded by his championship Yankee team after they won the first game of the 1999 World Series.

Postwar football players such as Dan Marino, Joe Montana, and Alan Ameche were perennial All-Stars, and by the 1980s the assimilation of Italian Americans into American life was so complete that little attention was paid to ethnic origins. Franco Harris, son of an African American father and an Italian mother, said he didn't know he was part Italian until he became famous as a running back for the Pittsburgh Steelers.

Although there were many Italian-American football stars, and prominent coaches such as Joe Paterno of Penn State, no one has left a greater impression on professional football than Vince Lombardi. Born in Brooklyn, Lombardi played football in New York at St. Francis Prep and Fordham University, where he became one of the "Seven Blocks of Granite" that manned the line in the 1930s.

After Lombardi graduated he coached at Fordham, West Point, and professionally for the New York Giants, but it was as head coach of the Green

A CLOSER LOOK:
A. BARTLETT GIAMATTI: RENAISSANCE MAN

Angelo Bartlett Giamatti was born in 1938 in Boston. His father, Valentine, was a graduate of Yale University and taught Italian at Mount Holyoke College, and his American mother was a graduate of Smith College. With such parents it is not surprising that Giamatti became a scholar. Dinnertime conversations at the Giamatti table often included such topics as Dante's *Divine Comedy*, and Giamatti learned Italian while still a child.

Giamatti majored in English at Yale, and graduated magna cum laude in 1960. He received a Ph.D. in comparative literature from the Yale Graduate School in 1964, and began his teaching career at Princeton University. He joined the Yale faculty in 1966, and in 1976 he became Frederick Clifford Ford Professor of English and Comparative Literature and director of the humanities in Yale's Faculty of Arts and Sciences. He held other prestigious positions at Yale afterward.

Yale began to experience serious financial problems in the 1970s, and was already operating at a deficit early in that decade. It was this environment that Giamatti entered as president of Yale in 1978. At forty years old, he was the youngest president of Yale in over two hundred years. Although reluctant to relinquish his teaching duties, President Giamatti successfully helped Yale recover from its economic decline, joking at the time that he would rather be president of the American League of Major League Baseball than of Yale.

Giamatti's baseball wish did not come true, but it almost did. He left Yale in 1986 to become the president of the National League, a post he held until 1989, when he took the next step upward to become the seventh commissioner of Major League Baseball. Unfortunately, he died suddenly of a heart attack only five months after becoming commissioner, and his short tenure was highlighted by his banishment of superstar Pete Rose from any association with Major League Basball, including the Hall of Fame, for allegedly betting on Major League Baseball games and associating with known gamblers.

Had Giamatti lived longer, he undoubtedly would have left behind a more positive legacy in the game he adored.

(*Above*) Vince Lombardi loved winning more than anything. As head coach of the Green Bay Packers he raised his hand in victory many times, savoring each win as much as the one before. Photo © Bettmann/CORBIS.

(*Right*) Joe Montana was instrumental in several Super Bowl victories by the San Francisco Forty-Niners. Many think he was the greatest quarterback of all time. He is seen here at the end of his career with the Kansas City Chiefs.

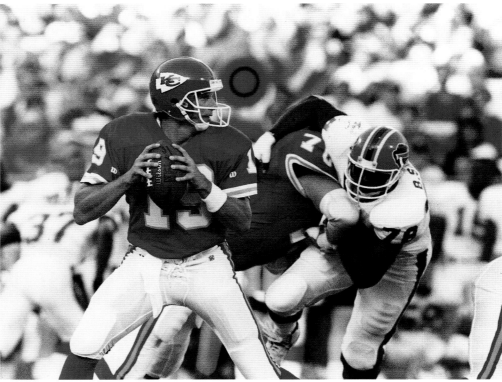

Quarterback Dan Marino was another consistent superstar, with the Miami Dolphins. He threw many a last-minute winning touchdown pass, and was the first quarterback in NFL history to reach 50,000 career passing yards.

Bay Packers that he established a higher level for professional football. His Packer teams won five Super Bowl championships in the 1960s, and set an indelible standard for future players and coaches. The Super Bowl trophy is now called the "Vince Lombardi trophy."

Coincidentally, both commissioners of the National Football League have been Italian Americans: Pete Rozelle and Paul Tagliabue.

The relentless pursuit of excellence shown by sports figures such as Joe DiMaggio and Vince Lombardi is one of the most important characteristics of hard-working Italian Americans in all fields. Two of the greatest Italian-American boxers of the postwar era were Rocky Graziano and Rocky Marciano. Graziano was born on New York's Lower East Side as Thomas Rocco Barbella. Street fights led him to reform school and the U.S. Army, but fortunately he was able to channel his angry energy into professional boxing. He went on to become the middleweight champion in 1947, showing his indomitable capacity to take punishment and still survive, smiling all the way.

Rocky Marciano became the undefeated heavyweight champion in 1952. His background was a little different from Graziano's, but it still reflected the intense desire to rise up out of a poor urban background. He was born Rocco Francis Marchigiano, and grew up in Brockton, Massachusetts, near the factory towns where so much Italian-American history is rooted.

University of Kentucky basketball coach Rick Pitino discusses strategy with guard Anthony Epps during the final game of the NCAA Final Four Championships in 1996. Kentucky beat Syracuse in the game, 76–67. Pitino went on to coach the Boston Celtics in the professional National Basketball Association; Boston is his home town.

Marciano's first love was baseball, but when he turned to boxing he exhibited his ancestral peasant characteristics in his tenacious style of fighting. There was much of the transplanted Italian peasant in Marciano—patience, the capacity to absorb punishment while dishing it out, loyalty to family and friends, and the ability to endure. He voluntarily left the boxing world in 1956 as the undefeated heavyweight champion. As a wealthy man who distrusted banks, he had squirreled away thousands of dollars that were never found after his death in a plane crash in 1969.

Basketball's Hall of Fame contains the Italian-American players Al Cervi, Forrest DiBernardi, Tom Gola, and Hank Lusetti, and coaches Lou Carnesecca and Hank Iba. Other Italian-American basketball coaches include Jim Valvano and Rick Pitino.

Favored welterweight Billy Arnold is knocked half out of the ring by a scrappy Rocky Graziano during their 1945 bout. Graziano won in the third round. Two years later, Graziano became the middleweight champion.

Arturo Toscanini (1867–1957) was one of the great classical conductors of the first half of the twentieth century, and his romantic orchestral recordings, especially of Beethoven, Verdi, and Wagner, are still prized today. Photo © UPI/Corbis-Bettmann.

ENTERTAINMENT

The world of classical music includes violinists Ruggiero Ricci and Nadja Salerno-Sonnenberg, ballet dancer Edward Vilella, composers John Corigliano and Gian Carlo Menotti, Dario Soria, the founder of Angel Records and for many years the managing director of the Metropolitan Opera Guild, and Joseph Volpe, the general manager of the Metropolitan Opera. Volpe's story is interesting because he started his career with the Met in 1964 as an apprentice carpenter. Since then, Volpe has worked his way up the ladder (literally) to master carpenter, technical director, and since 1990, general manager.

Some of the many outstanding Italian-Americans in the world of popular music are Sonny Bono, Perry Como, Vic Damone (Vito Farinola), Bobby Darin, (Walden Robert Cassotto), Eydie Gorme (Edith Gormezano), Connie Francis (Concetta Franconero), Jon Bon Jovi, Mario Lanza (Alfredo Cocozz), Madonna (Madonna Louise Ciccone), composer Henry Mancini, Al Martino, Bernadette Peters (Bernadette Lazzaro), Bruce Springsteen (half Italian), Frankie Valle (Frank Castelluccio), and one of the first "crooners," Russ Columbo.

And the jazz world is richer for the contributions of pianist Lennie Tristano, guitarists Tony Mottola and Pat Martino, bassist Scott LaFaro, and trumpeter Chuck Mangione.

Hollywood and show business in general were other natural magnets for Italian Americans, and in the early years of silent motion pictures the great-

Rudolph Valentino was one of the first and greatest sex symbols of the silent movies. His followers created a cult that still worships at the celluloid shrine of *The Sheik.*

A CLOSER LOOK:
FRANK SINATRA: THE CHAIRMAN OF THE BOARD

Frank Sinatra liked to refer to himself as a "saloon singer." No singer of songs has ever held the spotlight for so long. He started his career in 1935 singing with the Hoboken Four on Major Bowes Original Amateur Hour, which led to a national tour. Two years later, solo, he began his professional career as a singing waiter at the Rustic Cabin in Englewood, New Jersey. Harry James discovered him there and hired him as his band singer before adding him to the Harry James orchestra in 1939, when he made his first commercial studio recording. Frank was twenty-three years old.

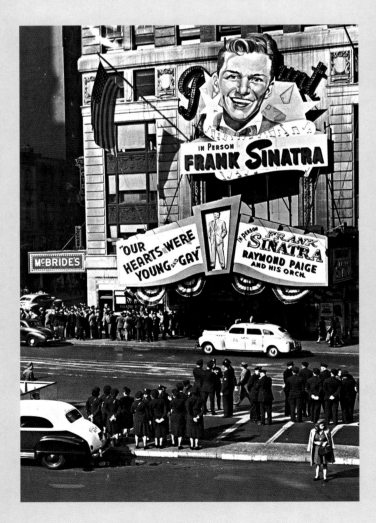

Sinatra joined Tommy Dorsey and his orchestra in 1940, and left in 1942 to pursue his unrivaled career as a soloist. He would keep on singing for more than fifty years, with one short "retirement" in 1970, from which he returned as the reinvented "Ol' Blue Eyes." He was good at reinventing himself, adapting and changing and growing, learning and even teaching along the way. He influenced everybody, even great jazz musicians like Lester Young and Miles Davis. Other singers sang the notes; Frank Sinatra sang the

meaning. He made you listen to a song for the first time, even if you had heard it a hundred times. He invited you to listen to the song *his way*, and listening to a Frank Sinatra recording is like looking at yourself in a mirror—you are hearing him, but you are seeing yourself.

And he made it sound so effortless, like Joe DiMaggio making a great catch or Robert DeNiro becoming a taxi driver for one hour and fifty-three minutes on the screen, and in your mind forever. Sinatra took his job seriously, and no one will ever sing a saloon song better.

Frank Sinatra was born in the Italian section of Hoboken, New Jersey, on December 12, 1915, and died a million miles away in Palm Springs, California, on May 14, 1998.

(*Above*) Tony Bennett, born Anthony Benedetto in an Italian section of Queens, New York, has been one of the world's most popular singers for more than forty years. He is also an accomplished artist.

(*Left*) Russ Columbo had already become one of the world's most popular entertainers when he died in 1934 at the age of twenty-six. He may have been the original "crooner," and certainly set the stage for other popular male singers such as Bing Crosby and Frank Sinatra.

est star was Rudolph Valentino, who was born in Italy in 1895 and came to the United States in 1913. Young American men like those who spent their evening hours in the dance halls of Second Avenue in New York imitated Valentino's every seductive move.

Valentino was born Rodolfo d'Antonguolia in 1895, in Castellaneta in southern Italy. He emigrated to the United States when he was eighteen, and worked as a dishwasher, janitor, and clerk in an Italian grocery. His version of the tango on Saturday nights in those Second Avenue cabarets, he established his early image as a dancing gigolo, and while touring the country as a tango dancer he was discovered in the bar of the Los Angeles Alexander Hotel. In 1921, the scriptwriter June Mathis suggested him for the role of the tango-dancing Julio in the silent movie *Four Horsemen of the Apocalypse* (which contained a legendary tango scene) and the rest was history. Valentino had become an overnight idol and movie star. With his next two movies, *The Sheik* in 1921 and *Blood and Sand* in 1922, he became a legend.

Perry Como was the most-watched popular singer on television for a long time. His mellow and sincere voice, his relaxed ways, good looks, and quiet sense of humor were what many people were looking for to bridge the gap between Crosby and Sinatra in the "Battle of the Baritones." He is shown here in 1957 with a young contender, Julius LaRosa.

A CLOSER LOOK:
CAPRACORN

Francesco (Frank) Capra was born in Bisaquino, Sicily, in 1897, and came to California with his parents when he was three years old. His father worked as a fruit picker in the San Fernando Valley in Los Angeles, and when Frank was old enough he also picked fruit, accompanying his six siblings. But in 1915 he entered the California Institute of Technology, studying chemical engineering. In the Italian tradition, he kept on working, paying for college by playing the banjo in local cabarets, waiting on tables, and working at the municipal power plant for twenty-five cents an hour.

When Capra graduated in 1919 he was unable to find a job, and for a few years he hitchhiked and hopped trains around the country. His break came in San Francisco, where he met Walter Montague, an old Shakespearean actor, who hired Capra to make small "poetic" films. After a year or two of too much aimless "poetry," Capra returned to Los Angeles and Hollywood, where he wrote gags for the silent-movie director Mack Sennett and

began to work as a freelance director. One of the greatest directorial careers had begun.

Capra's first big hit was *It Happened One Night* in 1934. It starred Clark Gable and Claudette Colbert, and won Academy Awards for best picture, best actor, best actress, and best director. In other words, it was a sweep.

Over Capra's long career he produced and directed such popular films as *Mr. Deeds Goes to Town* (1936, best director); *You Can't Take It With You* (1938, best picture, best director); *Mr. Smith Goes to Washington* (1939); *Meet John Doe* (1941); and one of the most popular films of all time, *It's a Wonderful Life* (1946), which is shown regularly on television, especially at Christmastime. Capra made his last film, *Pocketful of Miracles*, a remake of his 1934 film *Lady for a Day*, in 1961. He died in 1991.

Capra's Depression-era films were aimed at lifting the mood of a somber nation by showing that money wasn't everything, the rich were unhappy, and that love, affection, and honesty were the things that mattered for a happy life—all basic Italian traditions.

(Right) Clark Gable and Claudette Colbert in a classic scene from *It Happened One Night*. This scene was one of the first (if not the first) to show an unmarried man and woman sharing a bed-room (with a separating blanket hung from an improvised clothesline). In 1934, when this film was released, even married couples were shown in twin beds.

(Opposite) Frank Capra on the set.

Although the public loved Capra's films, and still do, the critics thought they were sentimental, and dubbed them "Capracorn." The films showed a nostalgia for the less complicated time of childhood, and a distrust of those in power, a holdover from his Sicilian roots. In *It Happened One Night*, for example, the rich—personified by Claudette Colbert—are depicted as spoiled, unhappy people who are only redeemed by contact with caring "real people," as played so well by Clark Gable.

Capra believed in the strength of his modest, hard-working origins and the opportunities the United States gave to every humble immigrant. He once returned to his boyhood home and reflected, "This house had been built by…the courage of two middle-aged, penniless, illiterate peasants who had dared travel halfway around the world to meet the unknown fearful challenges of a strange land, a strange people, and strange language. And who slaved like oxen and fought like tigers to feed and clothe their children."

When Valentino died suddenly in 1926 of peritonitis at the age of thirty-one, thousands of fans came to pay their last respects. That same year, Frank Capra directed his first film, *The Strong Man*, starring Harry Langdon. Capra became one of Hollywood's best directors, and his pictures are even more popular today than when they were first produced.

Madonna (Madonna Louise Ciccone) has become a self-fulfilling, self-propelling force in the entertainment world. To her credit, she is an excellent pop singer and actress.

Also that year, 1926, James Frances (Jimmy) Durante was singing in New York City nightclubs as part of a jazz trio that included Lou Clayton and Eddie Jackson. Durante was born in 1893 to immigrant parents from Salerno, and was raised in New York City's Lower East Side. His father was a barber, and catered to politicians in Tammany Hall, but the young Durante was attracted to the entertainment world. He dropped out of school in the seventh grade and began playing the piano wherever people would pay to hear him. By the time Jimmy was twenty-three, "Ragtime Jimmy" had his own five-piece band. It was 1916, the beginning of the Jazz Age.

At about that time, Durante was becoming aware of the music of Dominic James (Nick) LaRocca, who founded his Original Dixieland Jazz Band in New Orleans, and was becoming known all over the world. LaRocca was born in New Orleans in 1889, of Sicilian parents. He taught himself to play the cornet and soon he was creating new rhythms that later became an integral part of jazz.

Jimmy Durante (affectionately nicknamed "The Schnozze," for obvious reasons) had a long career as a musician, singer (of sorts), comedian, and actor in nightclubs, stage, radio, films, and television. Italian Americans loved him.

Premier jazz musician Louis Armstrong paid his respects to Nick LaRocca in 1936: "Only four years before I learned to play the trumpet . . . the first great jazz orchestra was formed in New Orleans by a cornet player called Nick LaRocca. . . . His orchestra only had five pieces but they were the hottest five pieces that had ever been known before."

Jimmy Durante was weaned on Nick LaRocca, using the new jazz music as a springboard onto Broadway, where his trio played in Ziegfeld's *Show Girl* in 1929. With his new image as "The Schnozze," Durante moved easily from stage to film to radio. In Durante's act one could hear the voice of the immigrant mocking himself, butchering the English language. He set the role of the good-natured working-class Italian who would later be seen again in such character actors as Danny DeVito and Joe Pesci. Jimmy Durante personified the easy-going, big-hearted Italian who never let himself float above his countrymen. He was the only celebrity to ever entertain the immigrants at Ellis Island.

By the 1930s Hollywood had begun to romanticize the image of the Italian-American gangster as part of organized urban crime. In 1930 Lew Ayres—a clean-cut actor who would later become the first Dr. Kildaire—was improbably cast as the first Italian film gangster in the flop movie *Doorway to Hell*. Then Edward G. Robinson scored a hit with his portrayal of the foppish Rico Bandello in *Little Caesar*. The Italian gangsters shared the screen with James Cagney, who played an Irish gangster in the now-classic *Public Enemy* in 1931.

Film director Vincente Minelli is best known for lush musicals such as *Meet Me in St. Louis* (1944), *An American in Paris* (1951), *Brigadoon* (1954), and *On a Clear Day You Can See Forever* (1970), but he has also directed such dramatic movies as *The Clock* (1945), *Lust for Life* (1956), and *Some Came Running* (1959). Photo © Alex Gottfryd/The Bettmann Archive.

In 1932 Paul Muni played a Capone-like gangster in yet another classic film, *Scarface*. The movie had an interesting background, especially as it related to the censors of the time. Unlike *Little Caesar*, whose hero was a swaggering braggart, *Scarface* introduced the image of the good Italian boy who loved his mother, defended the virtue of his sister while lusting after the "typical" blond American girl, and went down like a sniveling coward in a hail of bullets. Because of the pressure from the powerful censors it was compulsory to have the gangster die a coward's death, no matter how glamorous his life had seemed. Even Cagney, in

Angels with Dirty Faces (1938), went to the electric chair weeping, to show The Dead End Kids who idolized him in the movie that crime did not pay.

Italian Americans involved in motion pictures and television are almost too numerous to mention but it would be impossible to talk about American show business since World War II without acknowledging at least some of the talented poeple who have shared their talents with us: Don (Dominic Felix) Ameche, Anne Bancroft (Anna Maria Italiano), Alan Alda (Alphonse D'Abruzzo) and his father Robert Alda, Steve Buscemi, Lou Costello (Louis Cristillo), Tony Danza, Danny DeVito, Leonardo DiCaprio, Anthony Franciosa (Anthony Papelo), Annette Funicello, Ben Gazzara, Rita Hayworth (Margarita Cansino), Jay Leno, Ray Liotta, Robert Loggia, Ida Lupino, Dean Martin (Dino Crocetti), Liza Minelli, Sal Mineo, Joe Pesci, Susan Sarandon (Susan Tomalin, half Italian), Mira Sorvino and her father Paul Sorvino, Robert Stack (Robert Modini), Sylvester Stallone, Connie Stevens (Concetta Ingolia), John Travolta, John Turturro, and Jack Valenti, the president and CEO of the Motion Picture Association of America.

Liza Minelli *(center),* **the daughter of Vincente Minelli and Judy Garland, has managed to establish a well-rounded career of her own, winning an Academy Award in 1972 for her performance in** *Cabaret,* **a role she had also played on Broadway. Photo © Reuters/Bettmann.**

A choice group of Italian-American film directors—Vincente Minelli, Francis Ford Coppola, Martin Scorsese, Brian dePalma, Michael Cimino, Quentin Tarantino, and Stanley Tucci—have had a significant impact on how we have viewed the postwar world. *An American in Paris* (1951) is usually considered one of the best movie musicals ever produced. If director Vincente Minelli had done nothing else, he would still be remembered as a great director because of it. *An American in Paris* was light and breezy, but the contributions of Italian-American directors would soon change to a more serious mood.

A CLOSER LOOK:
FRANCIS FORD COPPOLA

Francis Ford Coppola's grandparents came from a region near Naples, but his own life in the United States was not typical of the immigrant experience. His father, Carmine Coppola, was a concert flutist who played with Arturo Toscanini's NBC Symphony Orchestra, and his Brooklyn-born mother, Italia Pennino, was a film actress. Francis Ford Coppola (the incongruous middle name came from the Ford Sunday Evening Hour Radio Show, for which his father also played) was born in 1939 in Detroit, but was raised in Queens, New York. After attending schools on music scholarships he became fascinated with film, and studied filmmaking at UCLA.

After film school Coppola apprenticed with moviemaker Roger Corman, and in 1962, at the age of twenty-three, he directed his first movie, a forgettable horror film called *Dementia 13*. But he followed that in 1966 with the remarkably good low-budget film *You're a Big Boy Now* (for which he also wrote the screenplay), and the block-buster *Patton* in 1970, which won Academy Awards for best picture, actor (George C. Scott), director, and screenplay, which Coppola co-wrote. But the really big movie came in 1972, with the release of *The Godfather*. Coppola did not like the novel, written by Italian-American Mario Puzo, and didn't want to direct the movie, but fortunately the producers persisted, and Coppola needed the money, so the movie, and history, were made.

Many Italian-American organizations protested the book and the film, which they felt denigrated the image of Italian Americans. Even as the film was being made the Italian American Civil Rights League demanded that all references to the Mafia and Cosa Nostra be deleted. They were, but no one was fooled. The film was a huge financial and critical success, and it helped create the image of the Mafia that persists to this day. *The Godfather* went on to win Oscars for best picture, best actor (Marlon Brando), and screenplay (Coppola and Puzo). In the pivotal role of Michael Corleone, Al Pacino established himself as a true superstar.

Coppola shifted away from the themes of *The Godfather* in 1974 for *The Conversation* and in 1979 for *Apocalypse Now*, a Vietnam war epic based on Joseph Conrad's novel *Heart of Darkness*, but his success (and notoriety) will probably never equal what he achieved with *The Godfather*, *The Godfather, Part II* (1974), and *The Godfather, Part III* (1990).

Coppola reflected the Italian love and trust of family when he cast his sister Talia Shire and his daughter Sofia in *The Godfather* movies and commissioned his father, Carmine Coppola (shown at far left in the family photo below), to compose and conduct the sequel soundtracks; Academy Award–winner Nicholas Cage is Coppola's nephew, and was helped in his early career by his famous and generous uncle.

John Travolta disco dancing in a scene from the 1977 film, *Saturday Night Fever*. The movie made Travolta into a star, is still popular on television and compact discs, and has spawned a Broadway musical and a Japanese movie imitation/homage, both the musical and the foreign movie still showing in 2000. After a hiatus, Travolta went on to become an even bigger box-office attraction in many movie roles.

After 1945 there began a flood of Italian gangster films, when Hollywood discovered that the "Mafia" was bankable. This trend reached new heights in 1969 when Mario Puzo's novel *The Godfather* was published, and the trend skyrocketed in 1972, when Francis Ford Coppola transformed Puzo's novel into one of the most popular and successful movies of all time.

Another Italian-American film director with deep roots in New York City's Little Italy, Martin Scorsese used his own experiences in his early films to capture the flavor of tough city life.

(*Above*) Actor-director Stanley Tucci (*right*) and Tony Shaloub in the 1996 film *Big Night*, which tells the story of two Italian brothers who come from Italy to open an "authentic" Italian restaurant in the Coney Island section of Brooklyn. Like most immigrants, their uncompromising efforts had ups and downs that finally settled into a comfortable success.

(*Right*) Sylvester Stallone and Talia Shire (Talia Coppola, sister of Francis Ford Coppola) in a publicity still for Stallone's incredibly successful *Rocky* films that began in 1976 and ended (probably) in 1990 with *Rocky V.*

A CLOSER LOOK:
UP FROM THE MEAN STREETS

Martin Scorsese, now considered one of the greatest film directors of all time, is the son of working-class immigrant parents. He was raised as a Catholic in New York City's Little Italy, and studied briefly for the priesthood before entering New York University's film school, not too far from his old neighborhood. His first film was *Who's That Knocking on My Door?* in 1968, when he was twenty-six years old. It tells the familiar story of a young Italian-American man who tries to reconcile rigid Catholic mores with the harsh reality of street life in Little Italy. Scorsese took a short step in 1973 to his second film, *Mean Streets*, which began his collaboration with the young actor Robert DeNiro, and continued his no-holds-barred look at young hoods in New York. The film put Scorsese (and DeNiro) on the map.

One theme dominates many of Scorsese's films, from *Mean Streets*, through *Raging Bull* (the story of Italian-American boxer Jake

(Above and left) A young Martin Scorsese (photographed in 1973) on the "mean streets" of his beloved neighborhood in New York's Little Italy, the setting and inspiration of several of the movies he has directed (and frequently appeared in).

LaMotta) in 1980, to the later *The Last Temptation of Christ*: redemption of sin through suffering and sacrifice. Scorsese continued the tough-guy theme in 1990 with *Goodfellas*, but switched to the classics in 1993 with *The Age of Innocence* before coming back to gangsters in 1995's *Casino*. He made yet another turnaround in 1997 with the epic *Kundun*, the story of the Dalai Lama, and is currently at work on a film called *Gangs of New York*, which promises to fulfill Scorsese's all-encompassing view of city life.

Since DeNiro's screen debut in *Mean Streets* in 1973 he has appeared in over fifty other films, and has even been the voice of Fearless Leader in *The Adventures of Rocky and Bullwinkle*. His acting range has spanned from a street tough to a psychotic taxi driver to a boxing champion to a classic Dickens character to a

tour de force comedic performance in *Analyze This*. He continues to grow as an interpreter of the growth of human character under difficult circumstances.

Scorsese and DeNiro have much in common—their creative collaboration could not have lasted so long otherwise—but two things in particular that unite them are an interest in showing character development, and their loyalty to neighborhood. Although they may not have remained in the Little Italy where they grew up, both are committed to bringing out the best of the city that has nurtured them for so long. To that end, DeNiro—the son of artists—is dedicated to his New York Film Institute in TriBeCa.

Robert DeNiro. Photo © Jeffrey Scales/ CORBIS.

TWENTIETH-CENTURY ART

Many Italian artists made their mark on the early United States, but the first of the modern Italian-American artists was Joseph Stella, who emigrated to New York City in 1896 from a mountain village near Naples when he was nineteen years old. He soon began to publish drawings of immigrants at Ellis Island, miners, and steelworkers. After returning to Europe for a few years, where he was influenced by the European Futurists and Cubists, he came back to New York and painted Battle of Lights, Coney Island, Mardi Gras in 1913-14, which an art critic called "the last word in modernism." His international celebrity was achieved eight years later, with his cathedral-like painting of the Brooklyn Bridge, *The Voice of the City of New York Interpreted: The Bridge.* Much later, noted art critic Robert Hughes said of the painting, "The bridge stood for the conjunc-

(Right) **Joseph Stella.**

(Opposite) **Joseph Stella.** *The Brooklyn Bridge: Variations on an Old Theme.* **1939. Oil on canvas. 70 x 42 in. Whitney Museum of American Art, New York. This painting is indeed one of several versions of Stella's paintings of the New York and immigrant icon—the Brooklyn Bridge. Photo © 1998: Whitney Museum of American Art, New York. Photo by Geoffrey Clements.**

A CLOSER LOOK:
RALPH FASANELLA: PEOPLE'S PAINTER

Ralph Fasanella was thirty years old when he painted his first picture, and he wasn't discovered by a major gallery and the general public until he was fifty-eight. Before then, he worked as a labor union organizer, a factory worker, and an attendant at his brother's gas station in the Bronx, New York.

Although Fasanella hadn't been *painting* all his life, he *was* looking —looking at everything in the neighborhood, from when he was a boy riding high on his father's ice wagon, or looking down on the bustling city streets from the fire escapes and rooftops above.

Fasanella, who died in 1997 at the age of eighty-three, delighted in painting city people in their element. As usual, it is Fasanella's city, his private version of the world around him. If you look hard enough you can see every person and every thing in every city.

(Below) Old Neighborhood. 1979. *(Opposite) Festa.* 1957. **Courtesy of Eva Fasanella.**

The painting *Festa* represents not one specific festival, but all street festivals that are so dear to Italian Americans. Festivals, usually called "feasts," are organized primarily to honor the Virgin Mary or a favorite saint, but the authentic Italian food sold at curbside booths is a major attraction for Italians and non-Italians alike, keepingthe festivities going late into the night.

Robert Venturi
(b. 1925), one of the
most innovative archi-
tects in the United
States. Venturi's archi-
tectural firm received
the prestigious com-
mission to design the
new wing of London's
National Gallery, shown
above in a model.
Photo © Reuters/
Corbis–Bettmann.

tion of old (Gothic stone mass) and new (steel cable);…it spoke of American unity, and still thirty years after it was finished, it remained the most
vivid and durable emblem of American technological aspiration."

Beniamino Bufano studied sculpture in New York and China, and in 1937
he was commissioned by the City of San Francisco to create the monumental statue of Saint Francis of Assisi, which towers over the city named
after the saint.

Another Italian-American artist with a Chinese connection is Mark di
Suvero, who was born in China while his father was assigned there as a
representative of Italy. In 1941 di Suvero moved to California and studied
sculpture and philosophy. In 1960 he had his first one-man show in New
York City, and in 1975 he had an exhibition at the Whitney Museum.

A totally different kind of art is represented in the "naive" paintings of Ralph Fasanella, who was born in the Bronx in New York in 1914. His mother and father emigrated from Italy and worked as a buttonhole maker and an iceman, while Ralph began to teach himself to paint while working as a laborer. He earned the respect and admiration of many as a self-taught social realist artist.

Other important Italian-American artists include Robert DeNiro, Sr., architects Peter Marino and Robert Venturi, and Joseph Stella's son Frank Stella, who launched the Minimalist movement with his stark black painting

Salvador E. Luria (1912–1991) shown receiving the 1969 Nobel Prize for Medicine from the Swedish prime minister. Photo © UPI/Bettmann/Corbis.

Die Fahne Hoch (Raise the Banner High) in 1959. He became one of the leading artists of the dynamic flood of abstract art in the following decades.

Finally, Leo Castelli was considered the dean of American art dealers for over forty years. He died in 1999 at the age of ninety-one, soon after starting a new art gallery in New York City.

SCIENCE

Antonio Meucci was born in Florence in 1808, emigrated to Havana in 1835, and came to the United States in 1851, settling in Staten Island. Considerable evidence indicates that Meucci invented the telephone before Alexander Graham Bell, but Bell is given full credit because he patented his similar version first.

Enrico Fermi is undoubtedly the most renowned Italian scientist to work in the United States. Born in Rome in 1901, he came to the United States in 1939, the year after he was awarded the Nobel Prize in Physics. His greatest contribution was probably his role as the leading scientist involved in the "Manhattan Project" that produced the first atomic bomb that shortened World War II in 1945. In 1946 the United States government awarded him the Medal of Merit, the highest civilian honor. Fermi received the posthumous honor of having the newly discovered element 100 named "fermium."

(Opposite) The contributions of Enrico Fermi (1901–1954) to modern science are incalculable, though he will always be associated with his seminal work on the development of the atomic bomb.

Another Italian-American Nobel-Prize laureate is Salvador E. Luria, who shared the prize in Physiology or Medicine in 1969 for his groundbreaking work in the science of genetics. Luria was one of many Italian Jews who fled Italy just before World War II. A multi-talented man, he founded and directed the MIT Center for Cancer Research, taught an MIT graduate course in world literature, and won a National Book Award for his popular science book *Life: The Unfinished Experiment*.

Poet Lawrence Ferlinghetti (b. 1919) reads from his works to friends in the basement of "City Lights," the North Beach, California, bookshop he founded in 1953, which helped foster the Beat movement of the 1960s. Photo © Roger Ressmeyer/CORBIS.

LITERATURE

Italian-American writers had begun early in the twentieth century to tell of the immigrant experience, and later, other Italian-American writers produced books continuing that tradition. The writers, who include Robert Canzoneri, Michael De Capite, Rocco Fumento, Lucas Longo, Joseph Papeleo, and Mario Puzo, were the children of immigrants. All of these books, with the exception of Puzo's *The Fortunate Pilgrim*, have gone out of print even though they were reviewed favorably. Even Puzo's book would be forgotten if his editor hadn't hinted that he would make more money if he wrote a book about the Mafia.

Among the other successful writers of the postwar period are Bernard De Voto, Paul Gallico, poets John Ciardi and Gregory Corso, and Lawrence Ferlinghetti, Jay Parini, and best-selling authors Gay Talese, Mary Gordon (half-Italian), Barbara Grizzuti Harrison, and Don DeLillo. Gregory Corso was known as a Beat poet because of his connection with the "hippie" culture of California. He overcame a turbulent childhood to finally establish himself as a poet committed to bringing about change. In 1999 DeLillo won the Jerusalem Prize, which is given to writers whose work expresses the theme of the freedom of the individual in society. He was the first American to receive this prestigious award. The following quote from DeLillo's best-selling novel

(Nunzio) Gregory Corso (b. 1930) is seen here sharing a comic book with his son in San Francisco, 1982.

(*Above*) John Ciardi (1916–1986), one of our poet laureates, was respected for his elegant language, his translations of Dante's *Inferno*, and several books for children.

(*Above right*) Mario Puzo (1921–1999), the author of the best-selling book *The Godfather* (1969), which launched four *Godfather* films. Many consider the Academy-Award winner *The Godfather* (screenplay also written by Puzo) to be one of the best movies of the twentieth century. Puzo is seen here at the premiere party for the 1972 classic movie.

(*Right*) Don DeLillo (b. 1936), one of our leading contemporary writers, has written many books. His 1997 sprawling novel *Underworld*, "a grand Whitmanesque epic of postwar American life," was nominated for a National Book Award.

Underworld summarizes the conflict that some immigrant parents felt about educating their children:

> Albert used to tell her in his slightly didactic way that the Italians of his experience, his Harlem and Bronx upbringing, his Calabrian heritage, tended to be wary of certain kinds of accomplishment, as immigrants, people who needed protection against the cold hand of the culture, who needed sons and daughters and sisters and others because who else could they trust with their broken English, their ten thousand uprooted tales, and he came home one day, the thirteen-year-old son, and saw his parents huddled on the sofa in one of those dolorous southern states of theirs, his mother's eyes dark-pocketed, drained by betrayal, and his father helpless and bent, a forty-year-old man who could double his age, in an eyeblink, through membership in some cooperative of sorrow, and they were looking at Albert's report card, just mailed from school, and he thought he'd failed everything, flunked out, been expelled, D's at best and funereal F's, but it was just the reverse, wasn't it, a row of A's with little gold stars stuck to the margins of the card, and young Bronzini eventually understood the nature of their distress, that they didn't want to lose him, the shopkeeper and the shopkeeper's wife, to the large bright world that began at some floating point only blocks away.

Happily, some things *do* change.

EPILOGUE

As the new millennium was upon them, the Italian Americans living in the United States could look back and realize that they had belonged to the twentieth century, and that those turbulent years had been good to them. Just as important, the Italian Americans had been good to America. In *lamerica*, over twenty-four million Americans with roots in Italy had found a good place to be, where the soft blue American sky would always nurture them through bright days and dark nights the way the soil of the *Mezzogiorno* had been unable to.

The big-hearted people whose names ended in a vowel had finally found out who they were and where they should be. The grandchildren of Italian immigrants could now say, not "I am Abruzzese," or "I am Italian," but proudly, "I am American." "I am me." And I belong.

July 4, 1986: The one-hundredth anniversary of the Statue of Liberty in New York harbor is enthusiastically celebrated by immigrants from all over the world. The lavish fireworks were designed by the Italian-American Grucci family.

ITALIAN SITES ON THE INTERNET

GENEALOGY:

1. The Italian-American Home Site
   http://www.italianamericans.com
   Comprehensive site including listings on genealogy, organizations, festivals, recipes, and links to other Italian sites.

2. PIE — Italian Genealogy, Heritage, Culture & Databases
   http://www.cimorelli.com/pie
   Includes information on Italian-American history, emigration, immigration, naturalization, as well as searchable online databases.

3. The Italian Genealogy Homepage
   http://www.italgen.com
   Extensive educational material ranging from an introduction to the subject, to comments on the meaning of Italian names, to determining ancestral nobility, to a civil records repository.

4. The Italian Genealogical Group
   http://www.italiangen.org/goal.stm
   A New York City–based group that meets on the second Saturday of every month from September to June, and is dedicated to furthering Italian family history.

5. Italian Genealogy Online
   http://www.angelfire.com/ok3/pearlsofwisdom
   A place where Italian Americans can research their ancestry, Italian surnames, and other family members around the world.

6. Genealogy "How-To" Guide
   http://www.familytreemaker.com
   Contains step-by-step instructions for locating different types of family information.

7. Italy WorldGen Web
   http://www.rootsweb.com/itagw/con/howtore/resindex.htm
   Includes a people-search, an overview of Italian Records, and genealogy books.

8. Tracing Your Italian Ancestry
   http://www.phoenix.net/joes/itans.html
   Simple advice on how to trace Italian ancestry.

9. Italian Genealogical Society
   http://users.loa.com
   A membership organization offering assistance in tracing Italian ancestry.

10. Italian Email Addresses
    http://mailory.tin.it
    Italian database of email addresses.

11. Free Genealogy Queries
    http://www.lineages.com/queries/queries.asp
    Unlimited free-of-charge genealogical queries.

HISTORY:

12. Windows On Italy—The History
    http://www.mi.cnr.it/WOI/deagosti/history/0welcome.html
    A complete history of Italy from prehistoric times through the post-war era.

13. Italian Historical Society of America
    http://www.italianhistorical.org
    Brooklyn, New York–based society dedicated to Italian history.

14. "When Italian-Americans Were Enemy Aliens—Una Storia Segreta"
    http://www.io.com/~segreta/index.html
    An online historical exhibit devoted to the internment, restrictions, exclusion, aftermath, and personal stories of the war era.

15. Timeline: Ancient Rome
    http://www.exovedate.com/ancient_timeline_one.html
    Provides a chronological index of the history of Ancient Rome with extensive links to internet resources.

16. The Italian Renaissance of the Fifteenth Century
    http://www.best.com/~natalew/zItalyRen.html
    Art history page exhibiting works of the major Renaissance painters.

17. Late Gothic and Renaissance Art in Italy
    http://witcombe.sbc.edu/ATHLinks2.html#general
    Extensive educational information on this important era in Italian art history.

18. The Florence Art Guide
    http://www.mega.it/eng/egui/hogui.htm
    A great guide for any visitor to the artistic hub of Italy.

SOCIAL COMMENTARY:

19. The Present and Future of Little Italys
    http://academic.brooklyn.cuny.edu/soc/semiotics/v1n1/index.html
    An essay about the current cultural and economical situation of "Little Italys" throughout the United States.

20. Affirmative Action, Defamation, and Discrimination Concerning Italian Americans
    http://www.italian-american.com/italaffm.htm
    Contains a large number of articles regarding these social and political issues.

ITALIAN-AMERICAN CULTURE:

21. Made★In★Italy★Online
    http://www.made-in-Italy.com
    A site that houses a plethora of information and links on current culture—from fashion & design to food & wine to shopping to travel to virtual-art galleries.

22. H-ItAM: Italian-American Studies
    http://www2.h-net.msu.edu/itam
    Subscription-based interactive network and forum for scholars and activists relating to the Italian-American experience and ethnic culture.

23. Lou Alfano's Homepage — Featuring Italian Culture and History
    http://www.geocities.com/Athens/Acropolis/1709/Alfanol.htm
    Contains interesting facts about the Italian-American experience.

24. Arduini & Pizzo: An Italian-American Family History
    http://www.arduini.net
    A family web site that has a wide scope of cultural information and extensive links to just about anything Italian.

25. Virtual Italy
    http://www.virtualitalia.com
    A cultural network filled with information and links to other Italian sites.

ASSOCIATIONS & ORGANIZATIONS:

26. The National Italian-American Foundation Home Page
    http://www.niaf.org
    The main Washington advocate for the country's fifth largest ethnic group.

27. Embassy of Italy in the United States
    http://www.italyemb.org
    Based in Washington, this embassy provides useful links and information regarding Italian activities in the United States, tips for travelers, a virtual newsstand, and economic, trade, and statistical data.

28. American Italian Heritage Association
    http://matrix.crosswinds.net/~capucina/AIHA.html
    Membership provides a sixteen-page bi-monthly newsletter filled with information on Italian Americans who have made valuable contributions to Italian heritage and culture.

29. Order Sons of Italy in America
    http://www.osia.org
    The official site of one of the most prominent societies for Italian Americans.

30. The Dante Alighieri Society of Massachusetts
    http://www.dantealighieri.net/cambridge
    An organization that promotes Italian culture by fostering achievements in art, literature, and science, as well as the study of Italian, and other cultural activities.

31. Italian-American Clubs and Organizations
    http://www.italianclubs.com
    Handy directory of links to Italian history, culture, festivals, and businesses.

32. The Italian Cultural Society of Washington, D.C.
    http://www.italianculturalsociety.org
    A non-profit organization that creates opportunities to explore Italian culture, and to strengthen bonds between the Italian and American people.

ITALIAN FESTIVALS:

33. Italian Street Parties, Festivals, and Good-Time Gatherings
    http://www.hostetler.net/italy.htm
    A free database (in English) of events, festival, markets, and celebrations occurring throughout Italy that can be very useful in vacation planning.

34. Italia Unita
    http://Italiaunita.org
    The organization responsible for East Boston's largest Italian festival. The site also contains links to Italian dining and wedding parties.

35. Italian Film Festival
    http://www.italianfilm.com

A festival of six recent and classic Italian films held every October-November in California.

36. Italian Festival of McAlester, Oklahoma
    http://www.italianfestival.org
    Annual festival information, events, and attractions, as well as links to other organizations and Italian festivals.

FOOD & WINE:

37. Italia Mia—Italian Cuisine
    http://www.italiamia.com/cuisine.html
    Selected Italian web sites on cuisine, recipes, wine, and more.

38. Italian Cuisine
    http://Italianfood.about.com/food/Italianfood
    About.com's guide to Italian cuisine, including recipes, restaurants, beverages, and extensive links.

39. Made in Italy Wine & Food, Wine Index
    http://www.made-in-Italy.com/winefood/wine.htm
    A clear and simple index of Italian wine—history, grapes, regions, wine museums, and books about wines.

MUSIC:

40. Italian Music
    http://www.italink.on.ca
    Offers a wide selection of Italian songs and music, ranging from folk to children's songs, and also offers promotional items, posters, and Italian tour information.

41. Italian Songs for Downloading
    http://www.geocities.com/SoHo/Canvas/9637/index.html
    Downloadable Italian folk songs, which change periodically.

42. Italian Music on the Net
    http://usa.musicaitaliana.com
    A comprehensive entry point into Italian music, this page provides an English search engine that can locate just about any Italian recording artist.

43. Italian Music Homepage
    http://www.cilea.it/music/entrance.htm
    Information about musical heritage, education, performances, production, institutions, events, and people.

44. Meri's Italian Folksinging Page
    http://pages.hotbot.com/arts/italfolk/home.html
    Contains the lyrics to hundreds of Italian folk songs.

LITERATURE & FILM:

45. Italian Literature
    http://www.crs4.it/HTML/Literature.html
    This site features the complete text of many classic Italian literary works and is compiled in Italian.

46. Italia Mia—Italian Cinema
    http://www.italiamia.com/cinema.html
    Selected links to Italian cinema web sites and videos on sale.

47. Italian-American Short Film Night
http://www.moondelabeam.com
A festival promoting non-stereotypical images of Italian Americans and the work of emerging Italian-American actors, writers, and directors.

MAGAZINES AND BOOKS:

48. Italy Italy
http://www.Italyitalymagazine.com
A bi-monthly magazine published in Rome, but intended for an American audience. Featured articles include Italian politics, culture, and cuisine.

49. The Magazine of La Cucina Italiana
http://www.piacere.com
A magazine highlighting Italian Cuisine, but also including articles on events, festivals, and travel.

50. Auto Italia
http://auto-italia.co.uk
A magazine entirely devoted to Italian automobiles.

51. The Italian-American Web Site of New York
http://www.Italian-american.com
A wide variety of links to Italian magazines, books, poetry, and newspapers.

LANGUAGE RESOURCES:

52. Italian Language
http://Italian.about.com/homework/Italian
Includes Italian lessons, chats, and other resources for the study of the language.

53. Cyber Italian — Interactive Italian Language Course
http://www.cyberitalian.com
The course teaches the language as well as culture, cinema, literature, and art.

54. Mama's Learn To Speak Italian
http://www.eat.com/learn-italian
Down-home Italian lessons, phrases, and recipes.

55. Travlang
http://www.travlang.com
A bi-monthly audio magazine designed to increase language proficiency and knowledge of current cultural and historical events (select Italian from the language menu).

56. Italian Language Learning Resources
http://www.call.gov
A collection of Italian language learning resources and links for Italian teachers and learners.

TRAVEL & MAPS:

57. Travel Europe Guide to Italy
http://www.traveleurope.it/Italy
Along with links to over four thousand web pages on history, tourism, and many other topics, this comprehensive travel site offers online booking and special offers.

58. Real Italy
http://www.realitaly.com
Tour Italy with the help of color photos and information on travel, dining, history, art, and more. The site also has a chat room.

59. Italy Tour
http://www.italytour.com
Take the ultimate virtual tour of Italy on this site. Visit restaurants and hotels in the famous regions of Florence, Venice, and Rome without leaving home.

60. Italy's Hotel Directory
http://www.italy-hotel.com/index.html
Search the most frequently visited destinations in Italy for available hotel rooms, or search by region or by province with the help of this directory.

61. Italy Map
http://www.lonelyplanet.com.au/dest/eur/graphics/map-ita.htm
Italy, Sardinia, and Sicily comprise the map. Interactive functions access more detailed maps in selected cities, as well as overviews of regional culture and attractions.

GENERAL ITALIAN SEARCH-ENGINE SITES:

62. Search Italia
http://www.searchitalia.com
Search Italia is a web directory and search engine of all things Italian on the Internet.

63. Tricolore—The Home of Italians on the Net
http://www.tricolore.net
A site including links to Italian culture, genealogy, business, and photos that also features a chat room, a forum, and pen pals.

64. Hugh Lauter Levin Associates Italian Links
http://www.hlla.com/reference/italian-links.html
The list of links from this very book is on the publisher's web site so you can go to our page and click on any of them.

INDEX

Page numbers in *italics* refer to illustrations.

PHOTO CREDITS

Courtesy the Aldrich Public Library, Barre, VT: p. 97.

Alinari/Art Resource, New York: p. 27.

Architect of the Capitol, Washington, D.C.: p. 37.

Archive Photos: pp. 32, 34–35, 38, 51, 52, 55, 60, 70, 71, 75 (photo by Augustus Sherman), 112, 167 (top) (photo by Robert Chiarello), 167 (bottom), 167–168 (background) (Paramount), 168–169 (photo by Dan Coleman), 184, 187 (Sporting News), 195, 196 (Reuters/photo by Pat Benic), 197, 198 (bottom), 199, 200 (Reuters/photo by Mike Segar), 204 (left), 207, 208, 210, 214 (Fotos International), 215 (Agence France Presse), 216 (Paramount Pictures), 217 (top) (Fotos International/photo by John Clifford), 217 (bottom), 218 (top and bottom) (photo by Jack Manning/New York Times Co.), 227, 229 (photo by Chris Felver), 230 (top left, top right) (photo by Bernard Gottfryd), 230 (bottom).

Art Resource, New York: p. 24.

Courtesy Avery Library, Columbia University: p. 105.

Courtesy the Bank of America Archives, San Francisco: pp. 170, 172–173 (all).

Courtesy The Barnum Museum, Bridgeport, CT, Photo © Kathy Weydig: p. 117.

The Bettmann Archive: p. 212 (© Alex Gottfryd), 213 (© Reuters).

Bodleian Library, Oxford, Ms. Bodl. 264, fol. 218r: p. 20.

Brown Bros: pp. 80, 99, 153, 158, 179, 180, 192–193, 201, 204 (right), 205, 206 (bottom).

Courtesy Mario Carini: pp. 65, 104, 107 (left), 108–109.

Photo by Maria Carola: p. 176 (bottom).

Courtesy Robert Carola: p. 109 (top).

© Center for Migration Studies of New York, Inc.: pp. 116, 139.

Photo by John M Cerritelli, Prestige-Barkley, Stratford, CT: p. 110 (bottom).

© 1997 Lia Chang: p. 206 (top).

CORBIS: pp. 114 (© Bettmann/CORBIS), 141 (©Ted Streshinsky/CORBIS), 150–151 (© Michael Maslin Historic Photographs/CORBIS), 178 (© Jacques M. Chenet/CORBIS), 182 (bottom) (© Jacques M. Chenet/CORBIS), 182 (top left) (© Wally McNamee/CORBIS), 183 (© Bettmann/CORBIS), 190 (© Bettmann/CORBIS), 198 (© Bettmann/CORBIS), 219 (© Jeffrey Scales/CORBIS), 228 (© Roger Ressmeyer/CORBIS),

© Corbis-Bettmann: pp. 73 (© Lewis Hine), 83, 106, 113 (© Daily Mirror), 161 (© UPI), 163 (© UPI), 182 (top right) (© UPI), 185 (© Reuters), 191 (© UPI), 202 (© UPI), 224 (© Reuters), 225 (© UPI).

Courtesy Eva Fasanella: pp. 102–103, 222, 223 (Quesada/Burke, New York).

Giraudon/Art Resource, New York: p. 25.

Photo by Diane Hamilton: pp. 50, 122.

Idaho State Historical Society, Boise: p. 137.

Immigration History Research Center, University of Minnesota, St. Paul: pp. 87, 142–143.

Courtesy Institute of Texan Cultures, San Antonio: p. 39.

Italian/American Collection, University of Illinois at Chicago, The University Library, Department of Special Collections: pp. 128 (IAC neg. no. 55.70), 129 (IAC neg. no. 170.2), 130 (IAC neg. no. 10.1).

Erich Lessing/Art Resource, New York: p. 61.

Library of Congress: cover, pp. 12, 13, 15, 42, 59, 62, 66 (photo by Levick), 67, 68–69 (photo by Lewis Hine), 76–77, 78, 84, 86 (photo by Jacob Riis), 88–89, 93,

94–95 (all), 98, 100, 101, 127, 140, 144–145 (all), 149, 150, 155, 157, 176 (top), 203.

Courtesy Mary Pasqua Lukash: pp. 107 (right), 109 (bottom).

The Metropolitan Museum of Art, New York: p. 43.

Robert Mondavi Winery: pp. 174–175 (both).

National Archives: pp. 56, 74, 96, 118, 120–121, 124–125, 126, 131, 135, 138, 164 (both), 188, 220.

The New York Public Library, Performing Arts Research Center: p. 115.

Billy Rose Theatre Collection, The New York Public Library for the Performing Arts, Astor, Lenox & Tilden Foundations: pp. 209, 211.

The New York Times/Golf Digest: p. 194.

Scala/Art Resource, New York: pp. 7 (photo by Giuliano Valsecchi), 8–9, 10, 16, 18–19, 21, 23, 28–29, 30–31.

Courtesy Shiloh Museum of Ozark History, Springdale, AK: p. 47.

State Historical Society of Wisconsin, Madison: pp. 132–133 (neg. no. WHi(x3)11515).

Courtesy the Staten Island Historical Society: pp. 90–91.

Courtesy the National Park Service: pp. 81, 233 (Statue of Liberty National Monument), 82 (Ellis Island Immigration Museum).

© 1999 Bill Stover, Page One Pictures, St. Louis: p. 162.

Courtesy Barbara Trafficanda: pp. 110 (top), 111 (both), 165.

© 1999 Jerry Wachter: p. 189.

Western Archaeological & Conservation Center of New Mexico/National Park Service: p. 45.

© Whitney Museum of American Art, New York: pp. 146 (photo © 1997 Geoffrey Clements), 221 (photo © 1998 Geoffrey Clements).